DORSET
AVIATION
ENCYCLOPÆDIA

RODNEY LEGG

DORSET PUBLISHING COMPANY
NATIONAL SCHOOL, NORTH STREET
WINCANTON, SOMERSET BA9 9AT

Printing credits. Typeset by Maurice Hann and printed by F.W.B. Printing at Bennetts Mead, Southgate Road, Wincanton, Somerset BA9 9EB. Telephone 01-963-33755.

Publishing details. Published by the Dorset Publishing Company at the Wincanton Press, National School, North Street, Wincanton, Somerset BA9 9AT. Telephone 01-963-32583.

Distribution. Library and trade sales via Westcountry Books at Halsgrove House, Lower Moor Way, Tiverton, Devon EX16 6SS. Telephone 01-884-243-242. Fax 01-884-243-325. Send a C5-sized stamped addressed envelope for a current stock list and order form, featuring a wide range of local and military titles, including others by Rodney Legg.

Updatings. Information for future editions will be welcomed by the author, Rodney Legg, at Wincanton Press, National School, North Street, Wincanton, Somerset BA9 9AT.

International standard book number. ISBN 0 948699 44 2.

A

Abbotsbury crashes — Squadron Leader Terence Lovell-Gregg crashed to his death at Abbotsbury Swannery in a Hurricane of 87 Squadron [15 August 1940]. He had led his men against impossible odds, head-on into a vast "Beehive" of German aircraft that were approaching Portland at 18,000 feet.

Opposite, on the pebbles of the Chesil Beach, Pilot Officer Maxwell had better luck when he crash-landed Hurricane L1764 on the day the Luftwaffe blitzed Sherborne [30 September 1940].

ADDLS — Aerodrome Dummy Deck Landings, practised on a pad at Henstridge Royal Naval Air Station that was laid out like the deck of an aircraft carrier, with arrester wires for authenticity [1943-52].

AE — code letters of 402 (Royal Canadian Air Force / Winnipeg Bear) Squadron, flying "Hurri-bombers" and then Spitfires from RAF Warmwell [1941-42 and 1945].

AFS — **No.210 Advanced Flying School** of Training Command was formed at RAF Tarrant Rushton, bringing Meteor and Vampire trainers to join the tankers and trials aircraft of Flight Refuelling Limited [November 1952].

An Airspeed Oxford provided piston-engine experience and the school went on to amass a total of 36 aircraft.

The school lost a Meteor and its pilot over Oxfordshire but the trainee flyer was able to walk away from the only crash at the base itself, in which a Vampire was crumpled on take-off [June 1953].

Some 150 flights were being achieved on an average day and a total of 16,500 flying hours would be clocked up by the school before it closed [March 1954].

Agazarian — Armenian/French Spitfire flyer **Pilot Officer Noel le Chevalier Agazarian** [killed 1941] of 609 Squadron from RAF Warmwell had an impressive tally of kills. These were a Messerschmitt Bf.110 [11 August 1940]; a shared Bf.110 125 August 1940], a shared Heinkel He. 1 1 1 [25 September 1940]; a Bf.109 [26 September 1940].

Next day's success, 25 miles south of Portland Bill, was Bf.110 (S9+GK) belonging to Erprobungsgruppe 210, an experimental proving unit from Cherbourg that was taking part in an abortive raid on the Parnall Aircraft Company at Yate, near Chipping Sodbury [27 September 1940].

His last decisive day with the Dorset-based squadron, off Thorney Island, Hampshire, accounted for a Bf.110 and Dornier Do.17, shared with Pilot Officer Nowierski [2 December 1940].

He was then posted to the Middle East and lost his life when 274 Squadron was intercepted by Bf.109s over the Western Desert at Gambut [16 May 1941]. He is buried in Knightsbridge War Cemetery, Acroma, Libya.

One of the Spitfires he flew *from Warmwell, R6915, survives suspended over the main hall in the Imperial War Museum, Lambeth Road, London SEl. It was also flown over Dorset by Flight-Lieutenant John Dundas.

Air Defence Research and Development Establishment — at Somerford, Christchurch, first made national news with reports that it had developed a "death ray" [August 1939]. This was probably a cover story for the development of radar and other systems. Perfecting ideas passed on to them by the Telecommunications Research Establishment at Worth Matravers they built the mobile Type 15 ground-to-air radar antenna which was put into a field at Sopley [25 December 1940] and would enable 604 Squadron at RAF Middle Wallop to score their first radar-controlled interception that ended in a kill [4 March 1941].

AI (Air Interception) radar — developed by scientists at the Telecommunications Research Establishment, at Worth Matravers and Langton Matravers [1940] . It was fitted in the Perspex nose-cones of Bristol Beaufighter night-fighters and first proven operationally from RAF Middle Wallop [1942].

Air Safari — operated from Bournemouth (Hurn) Airport [1960s].

Airspeed (1934) Limited — aviation company, makers of the Envoy and the Oxford, which established a shadow-factory at Somerford, beside Christchurch Aerodrome [January 1941]. 550 of the twin-engined Oxfords would be made there, mainly for use as trainers. Production then concentrated on the making of Horsa gliders for the airborne divisions [1943-44] and conversions of Supermarine Spitfires into Seafires, with folding wing modifications, plus the pilot's canopy having all-round vision, for use on Royal Navy aircraft-carriers.

Ownership of Airspeed (1934) Limited was acquired by the de Havilland Aircraft Company Limited [1940] and it would be renamed Airspeed Limited [25 January 1944]. Though it retained its separate identity it made parts for the famous de Havilland Mosquito.

Airspeed's principal post-war hope lay in plans for the twin-engined Ambassador airliner which it had already sold, ahead of production, to British European Airways. Flight tests were ominous and the company was merged into its parent de Havilland Aircraft Company Limited [1951].

The Ambassador subsequently saw the skies, with British European Airways, in their "Elizabethan" class, honouring the new Queen [1952]. It was soon to be upstaged by the more ad advanced turboprop Vickers Viscount and production ceased.

Air Traffic Control Evaluation Unit — moved from London Airport to Bournemouth (Hurn) Airport [1963] and used the busy South Coast aero-drome to test new radar systems. Operated separately from the airfield's own air traffic system.

Airways House — at 4 High Street, Poole, being the offices of the British Overseas Airways Corporation [1940-46].

Air Whaling Limited — established by helicopter test pilot Alan Bristow for Antarctic whaling expeditions and based at Henstridge Aerodrome [1953-54].

Airwork Services — provided target-towing flights for the Fleet Air Arm, from Bournemouth (Hurn) Airport [1952]. Deployed the same types of aircraft as were currently on aircraft-carriers, plus the superbly versatile Mosquito.

Operated in association with the Fleet Requirements Unit, giving active retirements to a succession of famous ex-RAF fighters, such as the Gloster Meteor and Hawker Hunter, and a virtual squadron of Canberra bombers painted in yellow and black stripes. After two decades the survivors left for the Royal Naval Air Station at Yeovilton [1972].

Akroyd — Spitfire flyer **Pilot Officer Harold John Akroyd** [1913-40] of 152 Squadron from RAF Warmwell claimed a Junkers Ju.87 in a fierce dog-fight from which he was lucky to return to RAF Warmwell, having had the rudder of R6910 jam over Portland [15 August 1940]. That luck ran out during one of the most hectic days of the Battle of Britain, when Spitfire N3039 was crippled over west Dorset and burst into flames on crashing at Shatcombe Farm, Wynford Eagle [7 October 1940]. Though pulled from the wreckage he was suffering extensive burns. He was taken to the Dorset County Hospital, Dorchester, where he died the following day, and is buried in the RAF plot at Warmwell churchyard.

Alcock — the legendary **Pilot Alcock**, of Imperial Airways, took flying-boats to India. As soon as he was in a warm airstream he used to drop his shorts and fly naked. His autobiography had the obvious title — *I Flew With No Trousers*.

Alington — fighter pilot **Napier George Henry Sturt, third Baron Alington** [1896-1940] of Crichel House, Moor Crichel, was killed at the height of the Battle of Britain [17 September 1940]. He had no heir, so the Alington barony died with him. His memorials are in Witchampton church and on the war memorial there.

Allen — Spitfire flyer **Pilot Officer John Woodward Allen** of 152 Squadron from RAF Warmwell plummeted vertically into the ground at Field Grove, near Travellers' Rest, Durweston [29 November 1940]. He may have fainted because of loss of oxygen. No enemy aircraft was involved. As he was killed before he could complete a single operational sortie, Allen was not among those posthumously awarded the Battle of Britain clasp.

Allied Expeditionary Air Force — control of 38 Group Airborne Forces and its aerodromes at RAF Hurn and RAF Tarrant Rushton, was transferred to the air-wing of the Allied Expeditionary Force [1 February 1944] for the imminent invasion of Europe. AEAF was commanded from Stanmore, Middlesex, and Norfolk House, St James's Square, which was the headquarters of the Air Officer Commanding-in-Chief, Air Chief Marshal Sir Trafford Leigh-Mallory.

Altair — Catalina flying-boat, formerly British Overseas Airways FM, which left Poole Harbour for Trincomalee, Ceylon [17 April 1943] where she was handed over to RAF South-East Asia Command.

Alton Pancras crash — at Austral Farm, of a Hurricane of 56 Squadron from RAF Boscombe Down, which had been battling against the formation of Messerschmitt Bf.110 fighter-bombers of Zerstörergeschwader 26 that were attacking the Westland Aircraft factory at Yeovil [16.00 hours, 7 October 1940]. Pilot Officer Dennis Nichols parachuted clear but was taken to Dorchester Hospital after landing badly.

Ambassador — post-war airliner, ordered by British European

Airways, and manufactured by Airspeed Limited at Christchurch [1951].

Anti-Aircraft Artillery — batteries issued with heavy 3.7-inch AA guns, and then the ubiquitous Bofors 40-mm gun, defended the Bournemouth and Poole conurbation and the ports of Weymouth and Portland during the Second World War. Guns were also mounted around military establishments and aerodromes. Several American "triple A" battalions, of Anti-Aircraft Artillery, passed through Dorset [1943-44] and were deployed to protect Blandford Camp and Tarrant Rushton Aerodrome.

The 184th Auxiliary Anti-Aircraft Gun Battalion provided protection for the beach landing assault exercise area at Studland. It had 25 officers and 716 enlisted men.

Anti-Aircraft Co-operation Unit — its H-Flight was posted from Gosport to Christchurch Aerodrome to work with the Air Defence Experimental Establishment in countermeasures against German bombers [1 November 1940].

Anti-Terrorist Airport — Bournemouth International Airport, at Hurn, was designated Britain's standby airfield for the diversion and reception of hijacked flights [1985]. An area towards the far perimeter was allocated for the isolation of such emergency arrivals, and a team briefed for carrying out negotiations with gunmen or bombers.

Preparations were also made for the control and manipulation of the inevitable media attention.

Major anti-terrorist exercises followed [1988] with elite forces, spearheaded by an SAS detachment from Hereford, practising storming techniques on a parked airliner. Contingency plans were devised for the management of such an incident, under the national command of government officials, with Dorset Police providing manpower on the ground.

AP — squadron code of 130 (Punjab) Squadron, briefly flying Spitfires from RAF Warmwell [30 November - 5 December 1941].

Appleby — Spitfire flyer **Pilot Officer Michael Appleby** flew with 609 Squadron from RAF Warmwell. He put a Messerschmitt Bf.109 into the sea, off the Isle of Purbeck, after an interception with Green Section at 23,000 feet over Swanage [30 September 1940].

Argentina — an ex-BOAC Mark V Sunderland flying-boat from Poole, converted into a Sandringham-2 for carrying 45 passengers and sold to the Argentine airline Dodero. Flown from Poole Harbour to Buenos Aires by a BOAC crew [17 November - 25 November 1945].

Arne crashes — of a Messerschmitt Bf.110 (3U+FT) belonging to Zerstörergeschwader 26, the Geschwader named Horst Wessel after the Nazi writer of a militant anti-Semitic song which became a national anthem [27 September 1940]. Crewmen Arthur Niebuhr and Klaus Deissen were killed as it exploded above Salter's Wood, Middlebere. The kill was claimed by a Spitfire of 152 Squadron from RAF Warmwell. They had been taking part in an abortive raid on the Parnall Aircraft Company at Yate, near Chipping Sodbury.

Some of Purbeck's most dramatic dog-fights of the Second World War occurred during a busy afternoon in the Battle of Britain, when the Luftwaffe attacked the Westland Aircraft Company at Yeovil [7 October 1940]. A Messerschmitt Bf.110 (3U+BT) belonging to the 9th Staffel of Kampfgruppe 26 came low across the Frome meadows and flew into the gorse-clad slope of Hyde Hill, south of Stoborough [16.00 hours]. The pilot, Leutnant Kurt Sidow, and his navigator, Gefreiter Josef Repik, died in the fireball.

Heinkel He.111 bomber G1+ES belonging to the 8th Staffel of the 3rd Gruppe, Kampfgeschwader 55, was brought down off Patchin's Point [12 May 1941]. It had just destroyed BOAC flying-boat *Maia* and was hit in the process by machine-gun fire from ships in Poole Harbour and Bofors anti-aircraft shells from the mainland. Two of the crew were killed but the other pair survived.

Arnhem airlift — nearly a hundred gliders, towed by their Halifax tug-planes, left RAF Tarrant Rushton [17 September 1944] to join the armada of 300 Allied craft that were to land behind enemy lines in the Netherlands. Operation Market Garden was airborne and the Tarrant Rushton planes towed the British 1st Airborne Division towards the farthest dropping zone, around Oosterbeek, four miles west of the great bridge over the Neder Rijn — the Lower Rhine at Arnhem — which would become "the bridge too far".

AZ — code letters of 234 (Madras Presidency) Squadron, flying Spitfires from RAF Warmwell [1941].

**Anson: coast patrols
from RAF Warmwell**

**Albemarle: twin-engined tug-plane of
British airborne forces, lifting Horsa gliders
from RAF Hurn and Tarrant Rushton**

B

BA — squadron code of 277 Squadron, flying Air-Sea Rescue missions off the Dorset coast, with Spitfires and Walrus amphibians [1943-44].

Baillon — Spitfire flyer **Pilot Officer P. A. Baillon** of 609 Squadron from RAF Warmwell was reported missing in action after dog-fights with Messerschmitt Bf.109s of Jagdgeschwader 2, off the Isle of Wight [28 November 1940].

Balloon Gerard Heineken — the world's largest hot-air balloon lifted off from Creech Barrow Hill, Church Knowle [evening of 25 July 1975], in an attempt at the international distance and duration flight record which ended half an hour later three parishes away at Coles Farm, Langton Matravers.

The basket of the 140 feet balloon snagged four power cables, 25 feet above a field, and plunged the village into darkness. "It's a miracle we're alive," said Army balloonist Major Christopher Davey.

"It was twilight and we couldn't see the cables until too late. Three cables broke and the other one wrapped itself around our flagwires. Then the basket swung like a pendulum until we were able to break free."

The fabric of the balloon was hardly damaged and pilot Don Cameron was talking of a second attempt within minutes of the unscheduled landing. Also in the basket was French balloonist Comte Jean de Costa Beauregard.

Half a million cubic feet of hot air had lifted the balloon for its passage across four Purbeck parishes. They were attempting to beat the 334 miles record, in a 16 hour flight, set in the United States [1974].

People converged on Langton Matravers from miles around and police closed the roads to prevent any more from trying to see the huge but collapsed balloon. Major Davey, whose £1 million insurance had also escaped a close call, issued an apology to the villagers:

"We, the crew of hot-air balloon *Gerard Heineken*, would like to make a full apology to the people of Langton Matravers for the inconvenience and damage caused to them and their property as a result of our forced landing at the start of our cross-Channel voyage.

"We particularly regret breaking the high power tension cables that blacked out the area — and which probably saved us from careering over the cliff."

Balloons — see entries for *Balloon Gerard Heineken, Double Eagle II*, and *Saladin*. Also Loders crash; Moreton Admiralty Airship Station; Toller Admiralty Airship Station; Hatton Turner; Upton Admiralty Airship Station; Zero Airships.

Barker — Spitfire flyer **Sergeant Pilot John Barker** of 152 Squadron from RAF Warmwell was killed in action during the Battle of Britain [4 September 1940].

Barran — Spitfire flyer **Flying Officer Philip Henry "Pip" Barran** [1909-40] of 609 Squadron from RAF Warmwell lost his life in a Battle of Britain dog-fight, as the Luftwaffe attacked Channel shipping. He baled out from L1069 and was picked up from the sea, five miles off Portland Bill, but was badly wounded and burnt, dying before he could be brought ashore [11 July 1940]. He is buried in his home town, in Leeds Cemetery.

Baynes — aircraft designer and inventor **L.E. Jeffery ("Baron") Baynes** [1902-89] is buried in Swanage Cemetery, Washpond Lane, Godlingston. He built novel little flying machines such as an auxiliary sailplane with a Carden engine which, together with its propeller, could be retracted into the fuselage; as was displayed to the Royal Aeronautical Society meeting at Fairey's Heathrow aerodrome [5 May 1935].

He was pioneering ultra-lights, such as the two-seater, twin-engined Bee which was only 29 feet 10 inches in length and being constructed by Carden-Baynes Aircraft Ltd at Heston. The twin 40hp Carden-engined Baynes Bee was taken up by Hubert Broad on its maiden flight [April 1937]. It and similar frivolities would be squeezed from the sky by the gathering clouds of war.

The Baynes Bee, plus a finely sculpted head, are carved on his Purbeck marble gravestone at Godlingston.

Beaminster crash — of a Dornier Do.17 bomber, shot down at night over South Buckham Farm [February 1943]. Its destruction was credited to Wing Commander Rupert Francis Henry Clerke, flying a Beaufighter of 125 (Newfoundland) Squadron from RAF Fairwood Common, in South Wales.

The farmer, however, recalled a Canadian pilot arriving in triumph at the crash site to claim the kill. Not only was Clerke "very British" but he had received an Eton and Cambridge education.

Beaumont — Spitfire flyer **Pilot Officer Walter Beaumont** [1914-40] of 152 Squadron from RAF Warmwell successfully crash-landed at Spyway Farm, Langton Matravers, after a Battle of Britain dog-fight over the English Channel [8 August 1940]. A week later he claimed his squadron's first battle double set of kills, with two Messerschmitt Bf.109s over the Isle of Wight [16 August 1940]. He shot down a Messerschmitt Bf.109 at Tatton Farm, north of Chickerell, on the day that three German aircraft crashed in that parish [25 August 1940].

It was regarded as tempting fate that he drove out "in shirtsleeves and sweat" to the scorched scene of his triumph. He baled out as Spitfire R6831 was shot down, into the sea, eight miles off Portland [27 August 1940]. Posted "Missing in Action" in Spitfire R7016 [23 September 1940], having apparently been shot down over the sea. His body was not recovered. He was posthumously awarded the Distinguished Flying Cross.

Benbow — air hero **Captain Edwin Louis Benbow** MC [1895-1918] of the Royal Flying Corps and the newly created Royal Air Force was shot down near Ypres on 30 May 1918. Born at La Mortola, Abbotsbury, he is buried in the British cemetery at Duhallow, and has a plaque back home in Abbotsbury parish church.

Berlin Airlift — three Lancasters and nine Lancastrian tankers of Flight

Refuelling Limited, based at Tarrant Rushton, flew a total of 6,975,021 gallons of petroleum products into the beleagured western sector of Berlin when Josef Stalin closed its land links with West Germany [27 July 1948 - 10 August 1949].

The round the clock operation totalled 11,827 hours of flying time for Flight Refuelling, but at a cost. Returning Lancaster G-AHJW flew into a hill at Conholt Park, Andover, killing Captain Cyril "Pop" Taylor and six of his crew [22 November 1948], and Lancastrian G-AKDP force-landed in the Russian zone [10 May 1949].

The 652 staff at Tarrant Rushton were particularly proud to hear that at 4.15 sorties per "Aircraft Day" theirs was the "Peak Utilisation Factor" for any aerial contribution; American, British or French.

Bulk fuel deliveries were almost as essential as those of food in ensuring the success of Operation Plainfare (originally called Operation Carter Paterson, until it was realised that linkage with a removals company was a propaganda fauxpas). The outcome was decisive and lasting. Post-war patterns of occupation would remain intact, to the inch and the letter, until the collapse of communism.

Bermuda Sky Queen — Boeing B-314 Clipper flying-boat that took off from Poole Harbour on her final flight [12 October 1947], via Foynes, Limerick [13 October 1947], outward across the Atlantic. She made 1,400 miles and was then forced by heavy winds to abandon the flight off Newfoundland, ditching beside an American weather ship.

All 69 passengers and crew were safely taken off and the flying-boat was abandoned to her fate, sinking in the Atlantic Ocean.

Blake — Spitfire flyer **Squadron Leader "Mindy" Blake** of 234 Squadron at RAF Warmwell accounted for two Messerschmitt Bf.109s as his fighters escorted Blehheims of 21 Squadron that were bombing Cherbourg docks [10 July 1941]. Blake was then reported missing in action but later sighted by Sergeant Pilot Fox, alive and well and cheerfully paddling his dinghy in the general direction of the Isle of Wight.

Blandford crashes — an RAF Meteor fell at Blandford [13 February 1969].

Blandford Forum is a tightly contained urban parish and crashes near it were generally in adjacent parishes such as Pimperne and Durweston.

Several, however, cannot be located with any precision. These include the loss of a Short Stirling bomber [16 February 1942], identified as R9306 of 90 Squadron

Blind-Landing Detachment — moved to the recently opened RAF Hurn from the Royal Aircraft Establishment, Farnborough, and was merged into the Air Ministry's newly formed Telecommunications Flying Unit [August 1941].

BN — code letters of 297 (Army Co-operation) Squadron, flying Mustangs from RAF Hurn [1942].

BN (Blind Navigation) radar — pioneered by the Telecommunications Research Establishment at Worth Matravers and Langton Matravers, and first tested in a Blenheim bomber of the Research Section, Telecommunications Flying Unit, from RAF Hurn [November 1941]. Using an AI (Airborne Interception) Mark VII radar set, having tilted its centimetric beam towards the ground, scientists found themselves mapping Bournemouth and could distinguish its streets and houses from the surrounding landscape.

Boitel-Gill — Spitfire flyer **Flight-Lieutenant Derek Boitel-Gill** of 152 Squadron from RAF Warmwell claimed a Junkers Ju.87 "Stuka" over Portesham in the Luftwaffe's Adlertag (Eagle Day) attack [13 August 1940].

"Bottled Gull" would be promoted 152's Squadron Leader and lost his life in a flying accident [August 1941].

Boudard — French flyer **Denys Boudard**, with Jean Hébert, stole a Luftwaffe Bücker Jungmann biplane from an airfield near Caen and flew to Christchurch Aerodrome [29 April 1941]. They joined the Free French Forces. Boudard was still flourishing in the 1980s.

Bournemouth — the second of the town's Spitfires, paid for by street collections and fund raising events, handed over to 457 Squadron at Baginton, Warwickshire [22 June 1941]. Left with the squadron when it was posted to the Isle of Man [August 1941] but then transferred to a training unit at Grangemouth [October 1941]. Lost in a flying accident [16 March 1942].

Bournemouth — designed by Lord Ventry, the first airship to have flown in Britain since the loss of the R.101 lifted off on her maiden flight from RAF Cardington, Bedfordshire [19 July 1951]. The crew were Captain J. Beckford-Ball, Freddie Twinn and Flight Lieutenant H. Richardson; the latter took Lord Ventry's place because at seventeen stone his lordship disqualified himself from lighter than air travel, blaming his predicament on having given up smoking. The three hung suspended in a gondola for the twenty minute trip. "Stern-heavy" was the verdict on her handling.

Bournemouth Centenary Aviation Meeting — held at the newly laid out Southbourne Aerodrome, and celebrating the first hundred years of Bournemouth [1810-1910] rather than manned flight. Notable for big money prize events attracting pioneer aviators from France, in which Leon Morane flew off with £3,425 of the £8,500 prizes. Remembered for what the newspapers headlined as "THE FIRST FATAL ACCIDENT TO AN AIRMAN IN ENGLAND" with the crash that killed the Honourable Charles Steward Rolls of Rolls-Royce fame [12 July 1910].

Bournemouth crashes — Rolls (above) was the first of many. Henri Salmet was luckier, in a Bleriot biplane that tangled with a Tuckton tree [summer 1913]. Trainee pilots for the Royal Flying Corps were soon to crash around Bournemouth in some quantity and with inevitable fatalities. Bournemouth Aviation Company operated from Talbot Village Aerodrome, where the casualties included Second-Lieutenant Edward Rebbeck, son of an ex mayor and heir to an estate agency [24 April 1916], and the death toll continued after the move to Ensbury Park Aerodrome. Major John Lockock was killed when his Bristol Fighter hit a tree on the corner of Christchurch Road with Annerley Road, near the Lansdowne [16.00 hours, 22 July 1918].

More spectacularly, watched by hundreds, a Westland Widgeon collided with a Blackburn Bluebird beside the stands at Ensbury Park Racecourse, killing test pilot Major Laurence Openshaw [6 June 1927].

Bournemouth's first air crash of the Second World War was at the height of the Battle of Britain [15 August 1940] when New Zealand Pilot Officer Cecil Hight, in Spitfire R6988 of 234 Squadron from RAF Middle Wallop, was shot down by a German rear-gunner. Hight baled out but was fatally wounded, his stomach ripped open by machine-gun bullets, and lost consciousness before he could pull the rip cord.

He fell into the garden of Mr and Mrs Hoare's house in Leven Avenue, west of Meyrick Park. The fighter left a large crater, and one of the wings landed on a hedge in Walsford Road. Mr Hoare would lose his life a little later when a German bomb fell on his house.

Hight is buried at Boscombe Cemetery and has a memorial tablet unveiled by the New Zealand Ambassador in St Peter's Church [7 April 1943]. The town would name Pilot Hight Road in his memory.

An unidentified aeroplane fell into the sea off Hengistbury Head after machine gun fire had been heard. No one baled out [1 October 1940].

A Messerschmitt Bf.110 fighter-bomber crashed on the edge of the town and was claimed by Flight-Lieutenant John Dundas of 609 Squadron from RAF Warmwell [15 October 1940].

Anti-aircraft gunners took the credit for the German aircraft that crashed into the sea off Hengistbury Head [1 December 1940].

Fairey Battle fighter-bomber K9230 ditched near the same spot [28 April 1941]. Second Lieutenant Andrew Page of the Lancashire Fusiliers swam to the aid of the pilot but despite heroic efforts, which won him the George Medal, he could not prevent the entangled parachute from drowning him.

A four engined Halifax glider tug-plane, from RAF Hurn, crashed beside Bournemouth Pier during a period of intensive training flights in the run-up to D-Day [26 January 1944].

Nine people were killed when fully-fuelled Halifax bomber JP137, carrying medical supplies and ammunition from RAF Hurn in a flight by 1658 Conversion Unit that should have taken it to a base in North Africa, crashed on the Bournemouth suburb of Moordown [22 March 1944]. It had left shortly after midnight and failed to gain sufficient1delete height. The accident could have been much worse as the aircraft happened to hit one of the few pieces of open ground in the densely populated area, below Meadow Court flats east of Wimborne Road, though two civilians were killed by the widely strewn wreckage. Sergeant Pilot Dennis Evans also died in the explosion, as did the six members of his crew.

Bournemouth (Hurn) Airport — interim name of Hurn Aerodrome [1952], before it became known as Bournemouth International Airport [1989].

Bournemouth International Airport — formerly known as Hurn Aerodrome, which opened as RAF Hurn [1941-44]. Renamed from Bournemouth (Hurn) Airport [1989].

Bournemouth II Crest — Mark Va Spitfire financed by public donations and war-weapons events in the town, handed over to 54 Squadron at Hornchurch, Essex [21 March 1941]. It would have a good war, being handed on to a variety of units including the 82nd Fighter Group of the USAAF, and ended up in the post-war French Air Force.

Bovington Relief Landing Ground — satellite station to Portland Royal Naval Air Station, for its helicopters, coinciding with the untimely death of the Commandant of the Royal Armoured Corps Centre in a crash [14 May 1969]. Established on the edge of a tank training area (Ordnance Survey map reference SY 843 904).

Bowhay — Canadian flyer **Pilot Officer Bowhay** of 418 (City of Edmonton) Squadron was killed when a Mosquito fighter-bomber crashed at Alder Road, Poole [23 July 1944].

BR — code letters of 184 Squadron flying Mark Ib Typhoons from RAF Warmwell [1944-45].

Bradford Peverell crash — Sergeant Pilot Sidney Wakeling of 87 Squadron from RAF Exeter was killed when Hurricane V7250 crashed in flames at New Barn, south of the village, during a Battle of Britain dog-fight [25 August 1940].

Brazil — an ex-BOAC Mark V Sunderland flying-boat from Poole, converted into a Sandringham-3 for carrying 21 passengers and sold to the Argentine airline Dodero [November 1945].

Brennan — the five sons of **Mr and Mrs R.J. Brennan** of Worgret Bakery, near Wareham, claimed something of a record by enlisting in the RAF [1940-41]. They were Samuel, Eric, Peter, Archibald and Edwin, and their ages ranged from 20 to 33. The other two Brennan children were girls.

Bridport crash — at West Bay, in a forced-landing on the beach, the pilot, thinking he was over France, of a Heinkel He.111 of Kampfgruppe 100, the elite two per cent of German pathfinder bombers operating from Vannes, Brittany [6 November 1940]. It carried the identification code "6N+AH" and would prove to be the most significant and revealing of all enemy aircraft captured in the Second World War, yielding Air Ministry boffins at the Royal Aircraft Establishment, Farnborough, and the Telecommunications Research Establishment, Worth Matravers, with a priceless haul of aerials and related radio equipment. This apparatus would correct a misassumption about the frequency of the radio direction beam, and enable effective British countermeasures, in time to save the vital Rolls-Royce aero engine plant at Derby [8 May 1941].

Bristow — test-pilot **Alan Bristow** [born 1923], a Fleet Air Arm pilot [1943-46] who then tested prototypes for Westland Aircraft Limited [1946-49], operated Air Whaling Limited from Henstridge Aerodrome [1953-54]. His four Westland S-55 helicopters were then sold to the South Georgia Company, for whale spotting in the Falkland Islands Dependency, but returned each summer for their annual overhaul until their final migration to the Antarctic [October 1957]. Bristow Helicopters Limited became the aviator's main business [1954-68] and then British United Airways Limited [1967-70].

The Brit — named Spitfire bought for the RAF by the people of west Dorset and named after Bridport's river. Handed over to 308 Squadron [10 May 1941]. Transferred to 403 Squadron [28 May 1941] and then to a training unit near Chester, being lost at the end of the year in a flying accident [21 December 1941].

British Aerospace plc — as British Aircraft Corporation became, would inherit the 500-series and then make a 475-series of the 1-11 airliner at Bournemouth (Hurn) Airport. With the completion of the last of this line the factory closed, just a month later [June 1984]. Hopes of maintenance work were insufficient to keep it open.

British Aircraft Corporation — absorbed the Vickers Armstrongs works at Hurn which had produced the Vickers Viscount and the less successful Vickers Vanguard. Its mainstay became the new BAC.1-11 which was made at Hurn and took off from there on its maiden flight [20 August 1963]. The airliner would go into a 500-series, with the 475-series following.

British Aircraft Corporation was transformed into Bristol British Aerospace plc, as the government privatised its planemaking interests [1984].

British European Airways — flew passenger services from Bournemouth (Hurn) Airport, principally to Jersey [1961-66]. Operated Vickers Viscounts, appropriately as every other one had been made at Hurn.

British Island Airways — operated from Bournemouth (Hurn) Airport, principally to the Channel Islands [1970s].

British Overseas Airways Corporation — formed by amalgamating Imperial Airways and British Airlines [August 1939], under the chairmanship of Lord Reith, the founder of the BBC. Its sea-based fleet of Short C-class "Empire" flying-boats were moved, with their supporting facilities, from Hythe, on Southampton Water, to Salterns Pier and its club rooms requisitioned from Poole Harbour Yacht Club, at Lilliput, Poole. These became the Marine Terminal.

Water runways, called "Trots", were marked by lines of tyres and extended from the Wareham Channel, between Hamworthy and the Arne peninsula, to Brownsea Roads anchorage between the island and Sandbanks.

BOAC re-established the transatlantic air link, from Poole Harbour, in "Empire" flying-boat *Clare* [4-5 August 1940].

The corporation's "land" flights — those from the ground rather than the water — were also transferred to Dorset/Hampshire, from Lyneham, Wiltshire, to RAF Hurn [1943-44] The first of its land-planes to land there was a Mark I Lancaster, G-AGJI, which was the first civilian-flown Lancaster in the British Isles. It was kitted out as a transporter rather than a bomber and was without gun-turrets though it retained wartime camouflage.

Following tests with a Development Flight unit the first of what would become post-war civilian Lancasters, to be known as the Lancastrian, were then ordered [September 1944].

Avro York transport MW103, an RAF aircraft loaned for civilian use, was next to use Hurn and took off for Cairo, via Morocco and the southern Mediterranean [22 April 1944].

BOAC flying-boats repatriated prisoners-of-war from Japanese camps, with the first touching down to sensational press interest in the men's stories of degrading and inhuman treatment [18 September 1945].

Former Halifax bombers, in conversions known as Haltons, were operating the BOAC land-plane route from Hum to the Gold Coast and Lagos, Nigeria.

British United Airways — operated from Bournemouth (Hurn) Airport [1960s].

Broadwindsor crash — Westland Lysander R9015 of 16 Squadron dived into the ground, out of low cloud in the hills above the village [16 December 1940].

Brownsea Island Major Strategic Night Decoy — deception pyro-technics, at the western end of the largest island in Poole Harbour, drew 150 tons of bombs intended for the new RAF Hamworthy [25 May 1942]. In all this "Starfish" apparatus would claim a total of 1,000 tons of high explosive that would otherwise have dropped on the Bournemouth conurbation.

Bruneval Raid — organized and practised for in Dorset by Combined Operations, under Acting Admiral Louis Mountbatten at Anderson Manor and Poole, this audacious air-sea commando operation brought back a German Würzburg radar apparatus from the French coast between Le Havre and Fécamp [27 February 1942].

The raiding party jumped from 12 Whitley bombers and landed on top of the 400-feet cliff in deep snow. They took their objective with complete surprise and dismantled the equipment for removal by landing craft from the beach below. Its components were taken for scientific examination to the Telecommunications Research Establishment at Worth Matravers.

Würzburg operated from a parabolic aerial at 53 centimetres frequency (between 558 and 560 mHz) and had a range of about 40 kilometres.

Buchanan — Spitfire flyer **Pilot Officer James Richebourg Buchanan** [1915-40] of 609 Squadron from RAF Warmwell was shot down over Weymouth Bay in a Battle of Britain dog-fight [27 July 1940]. He crashed into the sea in Spitfire N3023 and his body was not recovered.

Burton Bradstock crashes — a Hurricane of 238 Squadron from RAF Middle Wallop was shot down in a Battle of Britain dog-fight and crashed at Bredy Farm, a mile east of the village [13 August 1940]. Sergeant Pilot Ronald Little escaped unhurt.

Both the machine and pilot survived when Sergeant Pilot Ernest Snowden crash-landed Hurricane N2646 of 213 Squadron, from RAF Exeter, at Burton Bradstock during another action-packed day [25 August 1940].

A Martinet from the Armament Practice Camp at Warmwell Aerodrome developed engine problems over the Chesil Beach Bombing

Range [12 March 1945]. The pilot crash-landed at Burton Mere, on the coast between Swyre and Burton Bradstock, but was trapped in the wreckage. Two pensioner heroes, Burton villagers Miss Harriette Evelyn Bendy (aged 68) and Levi Rogers (aged 65) ignored the flames which were about to engulf the aircraft. They untangled the pilot's feet and pulled the shocked airman to safety as his aeroplane became an inferno.

Beaufighter: Sopley's 'Starlight' and night-fighter airborne radar gave 'Cat's Eyes' Cunningham a classic kill over Shaftesbury

Blenheim: test-bed of the secret war, flying from RAF Christchurch and Hurn for the boffins of the Telecommunications Research Establishment, developing ground-mapping radar at Worth Matravers and Langton Matravers

C

Cabot — Poole-based Short "Empire" flying-boat seconded from BOAC to 119 Squadron at Invergordon and sunk by the Germans in Bodo fjord, Norway [4-5 May 1940].

Cambrian Airways — operated from Bournemouth (Hurn) Airport [1960s].

Capital Airlines — of Washington DC, bought 60 Vickers Viscount turboprop airliners that were built at Bournemouth (Hurn) Airport [late 1950s].

Caribou — Poole-based Short "Empire" flying-boat seconded from BOAC to 119 Squadron at Invergordon and sunk by the Germans in Bodo fjord, Norway [4-5 May 1940].

Cattistock crash — a £7 million Sea Harrier of 899 Squadron, on a training flight from the Royal Naval Air Station at Yeovilton, went out of control above the village [09.34 hours, 21 January 1983].

It narrowly missed homes in West End and Beech Tree Close and crashed into a hedge one field away from the bungalows.

No one was hurt. The pilot, 28-year-old Flight Lieutenant Kevin Fox, had ejected safely.

Asked about village reactions, a huntsman at the nearby kennels told television reporters: "There may be some complaints from old women of both sexes but there are many military families in the area and most of us realise that these things are bound to happen from time to time."

Mrs Sheila Smith of Ramsay Cottage watched the Harrier "flutter to the ground like a leaf". She met the pilot as he was about to be taken from Lankham Bottom, by helicopter, to the hospital at Yeovilton air base: "I told him that he had not hit anything and he was very pleased to know that."

Earth and fragments of wreckage were thrown on to the tiled roof of

Fred Wainwright's bungalow. He came out of his garage as there was a second bang and the fighter hit the hedge: "We had a quick look down there to see if there was anyone trapped but you just couldn't get near. It was one sheet of flame, an inferno with black smoke rising from the wreckage."

Police had to break into one of the bungalows to reassure pensioner Mrs Evelyn Ardagh who had been so frightened by the explosions that she locked the doors and refused to come out. "It certainly knocked the stuffing out of me," she said after receiving treatment for shock.

Cawse — Hurricane flyer **Pilot Officer Frederick Norman Cawse** [1915-1940] of 238 Squadron from RAF Middle Wallop was shot down in P3222 off Weymouth by a Messerschmitt Bf.109 [11 August 1940]. His body was washed up on the other side of the Channel and he is buried in the community cemetery at Cayeux-sur-Mer.

Chaldon Herring crashes — of Messerschmitt Bf.110 (3M+KM) belonging to the 1st Staffel of II Gruppe, Zerstörergeschwader 2, in one of Dorset's busiest days of the Battle of Britain [25 August 1940]. It became a fireball at East Chaldon and the two crewmen died in the explosion. The kill was claimed by Squadron Leader H.S. "George" Darley, and American volunteer "Red" Tobin in Spitfires of 609 Squadron from RAF Warmwell.

152 Squadron from Warmwell lost Spitfire R6607 at the northern extremity of the parish, beside Tadnoll Mill, when Sergeant Pilot Edmund Shepperd plunged into the ground [18 October 1940]. No other aeroplane was involved and there was no obvious reason for the accident.

Channel Airways — operated from Bournemouth (Hurn) Airport to Jersey and Guernsey [from 1966]. Its principal aircraft was the Trident.

Cheselbourne crashes — of Spitfire X4107, with Pilot Officer Mick Miller of 609 Squadron from RAF Warmwell, after his fatal collision with a Messerschmitt Bf.110 (3U+FT) at 24,000 feet above Bellamy's Farm, Piddletrenthide [27 September 1940]. Most of the wreckage fell to the east of Doles Ash Farm, on the Cheselbourne side of the parish boundary.

A Lockheed P-38 Lightning of the 474th Fighter Group of the United States Army Air Force, flying from Warmwell Aerodrome, crashed near Cheselbourne [21 May 1944]. Lieutenant Kimball was killed in the accident.

Chesil Beach Bombing Range — established along The Fleet lagoon [1937] and extended as the Lyme Bay Bombing Range [August 1939] with a notable wartime rôle that included the testing to perfection of the Dambuster bombs [December 1942 - March 1943].

Chesil Beach crashes — other than those listed elsewhere, under the specific parish entries for Abbotsbury, Chickerell, Fleet, and Langton Herring. Most misadventures were to users of the Chesil Beach Bombing Range and often those that fell on the beach itself and the adjacent mainland were listed and recorded as range rather than parish casualties.

Fairey Battle K7594 of 226 Squadron spun out of control into the Chesil Beach [11 December 1937].

Hawker Fury K8223 of 9 Flying Training School hit a drogue, caught fire, and crashed into the sea off the pebble bank [25 May 1938].

Hawker Fury K8271, also belonging to 9 Flying School, came down into the pebbles [10 December 1938].

Hawker Audax K4396 of 6 Flying Training School crashed on failing to pull out of a dive [13 March 1939].

Boulton Paul Overstrand K8173 of 10 Bombing and Gunnery School at RAF Warmwell crashed into the sea off the Chesil Beach [22 April 1940].

Blenheim L9405, a Mark V bomber, ditched in Lyme Bay, off the Chesil Beach [29 November 1941].

Chickerell Aerodrome — now built upon, at the eastern edge of the parish between the B3157 at Marquis Farm and West Haven Hospital, Westham, Weymouth (SY 657 793). It was a grass airstrip with a main runway of 2,400 feet and a hangar in the south-east corner. Established as Royal Naval Air Station Portland in 1918 with No.513 Flight operating DH6s against U-boats in the English Channel.

These de Havilland aircraft and their crews were reformed into 241

Squadron of the Royal Air Force in August 1918, being attached to 75 Wing of 10 Group. They were disbanded on 23 January 1919. Short-term civilian use followed, with Handley Page Air Transport flying ex-military 0-400s from Cricklewood, but giving Weymouth an air service was an idea ahead of its time.

Between the wars the aerodrome, which doubled as playing fields, was visited by Sir Alan Cobham's Flying Circus. The military lease of the land resumed in October 1936, through the Air Ministry, on behalf of Bomber Command. It was commissioned as the Forward Landing Aerodrome for the Chesil Beach Bombing Range, to act as a satellite airfield to Warmwell Aerodrome (known as Woodsford Aerodrome from its opening in May 1937 until renaming on 1 July 1938). The main reason for requisitioning Chickerell was so that aircraft in landing difficulties had an emergency landing strip within a mile of the east end of the range. As well as hosting the fire engine and ambulance it also accommodated range personnel.

K.S. West's researches have shown that Pilot Officer A.E. de Pencier, killed on 13 March 1939, was one of its emergencies. Martinet aircraft from No.771 FRU Squadron based at Royal Naval Air Station Gosport were at Chickerell from September 1945 until August 1955, a period when the Chesil Beach was used by Sunderland flying boats and other bombers. The aerodrome was derequisitioned in 1959.

Chickerell crashes — Lysander L2057 of 613 Squadron, on a training flight during the "Phoney War", crashed in the village [23 April 1940].

A Messerschmitt Bf.109, crashed into the Chesil Beach during one of the busiest days of the Battle of Britain [25 August 1940]. The pilot, Hauptmann Maculan, apparently fell out and drowned.

The same dog-fights accounted for a Bf.110 at Tatton House, west of Buckland Ripers, killing both crew. Then a Bf.109 belly-landed in an adjoining field at Tatton Farm. Its pilot, Gefreiter Josef Broker of Jagdgeschwader 53, escaped with wounds as the fighter was engulfed in flames.

Spitfires from RAF Warmwell claimed the kills; the first was credited to Squadron Leader H.S. "George" Darley of 609 Squadron, and the third to Pilot Officer W. Beaumont of 152 Squadron.

Losses on the Chesil Beach Bombing Range, other than those that can be identified with a particular parish, are listed in the entry for Chesil Beach crashes.

Child Okeford crash — at Netmead in the common land meadows west of the village, beside the River Stour, of Spitfire N3231 from RAF Warmwell [16.00 hours, 7 October 1940]. It was shot down in one of the dog-fights following the attack on the Westland Aircraft Company factory at Yeovil, and Pilot Officer Michael Staples of 609 Squadron baled out at 21,000 feet with what he described as "a big hole" in his leg. He landed without further damage and was taken to Blandford Cottage Hospital.

Chilfrome crash — Hawker Typhoon R8663 of 257 Squadron crashed in a wartime forced-landing at Chilfrome [15 December 1942].

Christchurch Aero Club — formed post-war [1950] and became the last users of Christchurch Aerodrome after the withdrawal of de Havilland to Chester [1962]. Flew a selection of Tiger Moths and Austers, plus a few Airspeed Oxfords that had been pensioned off by the RAF's Air Service Training arm. These were particularly appropriate, being returnees to the airfield where some of them had been constructed.

Other aircraft included Rapides, Colt, and Tripacer trainers. Gradually they disappeared as housing estates encroached but a photograph in Leslie Dawson's Wings over Dorset shows G.E.H. Gould's rebuilt Auster J1-N being fuelled at the Christchurch Aero Club pumps in 1972 — eight years after the airfield had been officially closed [1964].

Christchurch Aerodrome — RAF Christchurch, a grass airfield of five runways at 20 feet above sea level on a gravel plain at Somerford, to the east of the town (SZ 185 930), established on an existing leisure-flying field for the use of the Air Defence Research Establishment [1935]. The Special Duty Flight, attached to the Telecommunications Research Establishment, came to Christchurch when the scientists moved from

Dundee to Worth Matravers [5 May 1940]. They were protected by three
Hurricane fighters, L1552, L1562 and L1592. Became a major manu-
facturing base with the establishment of a shadow-factory for Airspeed
(1934) Limited [January 1941].

Airfield pundit code "XC".

As it expanded, Christchurch Aerodrome attracted inevitable attention
from the Luftwaffe, though the first wave of bombs exploded harmlessly
or not at all [10 May 1941]. The next raid hit nearby civilian buildings [12
May 1941].

The Airspeed factory at Christchurch Aerodrome converted 160
standard Supermarine Spitfires into Seafires, for use by the Fleet Air Arm
on Royal Navy aircraft-carriers [1943-45].

As preparations for the invasion of Europe gathered pace, RAF
Christchurch became Station 416, Advance Landing Group Christchurch,
of the 9th United States Army Air Force [7 March 1944]. Nearly a
thousand officers and men of the 405th Fighter Bomber Group arrived by
train from the liner *Mauretania* which had docked at Liverpool.

The 405th comprised 509, 510, and 511 Squadrons of the USAAF,
equipped with Republic P-47 Thunderbolt fighter-bombers.

For the people of Christchurch the noise, excitement and danger from
bomb-laden crash-landings would soon become a memory, as the entire
405th Fighter Bomber Group were ordered to follow the war across the
Channel and took off for Airstrip 8, at Picauville, in the Allied-occupied
Cherbourg peninsula [11 July 1944].

Christchurch crashes — Royal Navy Seafire MB315, arriving at
Christchurch Aerodrome from Donibristle, Scotland, overshot the
runway and crashed into a bungalow, "Musoka" in Caroline Avenue, at
Stanpit [25 June 1943]. The pilot, Sub-Lieutenant P.M. Lamb, was taken
to hospital with head injuries but survived to continue his career, though
he had to grow his hair long to cover the scars. "Not my best landing," he
wrote in his log.

An American P-47 Thunderbolt from Christchurch Aerodrome
crashed in the playground at Highcliffe School [19.03 hours, 30 April
1944]. The pilot had baled out, landing unhurt in the nearby recreation

ground, and the school was empty at the time of the accident.

An RAF Wellington bomber crashed near Christchurch Aerodrome, on the north side of the railway line [13.00 hours, 25 May 1944].

The worst air-crash of the war, for Christchurch and the rest of the conurbation and Dorset itself, occurred when Foxwood Avenue, Mudeford, was devastated by three P-47 Thunderbolt fighter-bombers of the 509th Squadron of the 405th Fighter Bomber Group. In the first mishap on take-off from Christchurch Advance Landing Ground, Lieutenant Vincent R. James survived and no one was hurt on the ground [06.45 hours, 29 June 1944].

Then at 14.00 hours the same pilot tried again to lift off. Once more he failed to gain proper height and this time overshot the runway into a bungalow. His fuel tanks and bombs exploded, bringing down another Thunderbolt that was coming in to land. Its pilot was unhurt.

Sixteen were killed and 18 injured in the accident and a subsequent explosion as a bomb went off among rescue workers. Mortally wounded, 20-year-old Lieutenant James would die in the arms of nurse Irene Stevenson, in Boscombe Hospital.

The next Thunderbolt mishap was less dramatic. A P-47 landed short of the runway and came down in a perimeter field, from where it bounced on to the Lymington road [17.00 hours, 2 July 1944]. It came to rest upside down. There was no fire, no civilian involvement, and the pilot escaped.

A lucky escape was had by men of the 306th Bombardment Group of the United States Army Air Force, arriving for recuperation at the seaside, when B-17 Flying Fortress 866 overshot the western boundary of the notoriously short Christchurch Aerodrome [15 July 1945]. It ploughed into scrubland, ripping out the near-side port engine, but came to a halt without exploding. No one was hurt.

The production prototype Airspeed Ambassador, G-ALFR made in the factory beside the aerodrome, came down heavily during a flight trial and lost both engines before it flopped to a halt [13 November 1950].

One post-war afternoon, just three days before the US Air Force bombed North Korea, a Fairey Barracuda of 750 Naval Air Squadron — one of four from the Observer Air Training School at Royal Naval Air Station St Merryn, Cornwall, that were taking part in Exercise Castanets

— crashed into Christchurch Bay, off Highcliffe [20 June 1952]. It had suffered engine failure.

The pilot, Lieutenant Albert Stanbridge, and his passengers, Midshipmen Thomas Penfold and Francis Kirk were able to escape in rubber dinghies. The three were picked up by a Sea Otter within twenty minutes. Rather than risking a take-off it then taxied to the shore at Christchurch from where the men were taken to Boscombe Hospital for a brief check-up.

More than a decade later the engine and the mid-section of the fuselage were winched from the water and taken to the Military Engineering Experimental Establishment [4 June 1968].

Two British Army Sioux helicopters of the Blue Eagles crashed at Christchurch after a mid-air collision [23 August 1969].

Christie — Spitfire flyer **John McBean Christie** [1918-40] of 152 Squadron from RAF Warmwell was shot down in K9882 by Messerschmitt Bf.109s off Swanage [26 September 1940]. He had been attempting to intercept the formation of some 60 Heinkel He.111 bombers that wrecked the Supermarine Works at Woolston, Southampton. His body was recovered from the sea and sent home, to Arkleston Cemetery, Renfrew.

Church Knowle crashes — a Messerschmitt Bf.110 crashed at Creech Barrow Hill during a day of Battle of Britain dog-fights [25 August 1940]. The crew parachuted into captivity.

It is also possible that the volcano-shaped mass of Creech Barrow Hill, swelling out of the Purbeck heaths, also claimed Short Stirling R9306 of 90 Squadron [16 February 1943]. The bomber flew into the ground in Dorset but conflicting locations have been given. Blandford has been recorded but Creech Barrow would seem much more likely.

Churchill — wartime **Prime Minister Winston Churchill** was flown in a twin-engined de Havilland Flamingo transport aircraft from Warmwell Aerodrome to Paris for secret discussions on the Fall of France [31 May 1940]. He was escorted by nine Hurricanes of 601 (County of London) Squadron, who saw him safely home the following day.

Later in the war, shortly after its opening, RAF Hurn was provided with a VIP hangar for the Prime Minister's personal Liberator and other special aircraft [July 1942].

City of Liverpool — one of the two Sunderland flying-boat hulks abandoned in Poole Harbour when British Overseas Airways Corporation departed for Southampton Water [1948]. *Solway* was the other.

City of Liverpool would be highest up the shore when the two fuselages were finally stranded at Lower Hamworthy, like beached whales [1958-59].

She had been built as Short's S.1297, became RAF serial number NJ205, ending her flying days as a Mark 2 Solent conversion, civilian call-sign G-AKNS.

Clare — British Overseas Airways Corporation's Short "Empire" flying-boat, which resumed the transatlantic air service between Britain and the United States, from Poole Harbour [4-5 August 1940]. Seats were at a premium, being reserved for VIPs on war service. Air Ministry Under-Secretary Harold Balfour would go on *Clare's* second wartime crossing — to buy three Boeing 314 "Clipper" flying-boats [14 August 1940].

Clio — Poole-based British Overseas Corporation Short "Empire" flying-boat, flown to Belfast for a military refit to equip her with four machine guns in each of two Boulton-Paul turrets, in the dorsal and tail, plus armour plating, bomb-racks on the wings, and radar. She became Coastal Command aircraft AX659 and was posted to 201 Squadron in northern Scotland [12 March 1941], covering the Iceland Gap, until being lost [22 August 1941].

Clyde — British Overseas Airways Corporation Short "Empire" flying-boat, which flew Colonel René de Larminat from Poole Harbour to Leopoldville in the Belgian Congo, to organize the repossession of French Equatorial Africa [5 August 1940].

Cobham — pioneer aviator **Sir Alan Cobham** [1894-1973], the first to make return flights to Cape Town and Australia, developed the flight refuelling techniques that would extend the horizons for long-distance flying. His post-war Flight Refuelling Limited was based at Tarrant Rushton Aerodrome and has its offices at Wimborne. Sir Alan retired to Falaise, a 1913-built mansion at 13 West Overcliff Drive, Bournemouth.

Alan Cobham flew in the Royal Flying Corps [1917] and after the Great War gave thousands of people their first experience of the sky with joy-rides in an Avro 504K. Then with the creation of the de Havilland Aircraft Company in 1921 he became a test pilot. He also flew 8,000 miles in three months on charter flights across Europe and North Africa.

Long-distance flying became his forte. Using a four-seater de Havilland passenger aeroplane, the DH-50, he became the first to fly over the Himalayas. On 16 November 1925 he took the adventure further, with the first "Air Route Survey" flight for Imperial Airways from Croydon Aerodrome to Capetown, which was reached on 26 February 1926. They were back in England on 13 March 1926, having covered sixteen thousand miles with Cobham being solo at the controls for more than ninety hours. Despite the prolonged stop-offs, necessary to sort out the arrangements of commercial landings, they were still able to beat a liner back to Britain by a day.

This first return crossing of the entire African continent earned Alan Cobham a string of accolades. These included the Air Force Cross, the Britannia Trophy, Royal Aero Club Gold Medal, Royal Institute of Transport Aviation Gold Medal, and the Royal Institute of Aeronautical Engineers' Simms Gold Medal.

Then on 30 June 1926 he lifted off the River Medway in a DH-50 fitted with floats and headed for Australia. The flight would have been a total success but for the trauma of what happened when the plane flew over what then and now is the most dangerous area of the globe. The co-pilot, Arthur Elliott, was killed by a Bedouin bullet as they crossed the Iraqi desert between Baghdad and Basra. The subsequent triumph of landing in Sydney was capped by a London homecoming at 14.05 on 1 October 1926 that took place in spectacular style. Cobham had landed in the Thames between Westminster Bridge and Vauxhall Bridge. He was then rowed to the steps of the Houses of Parliament and was greeted at the top by Sir Samuel Hoare, the Secretary of State for Air.

Within a week he had conquered the second bastion of the British establishment and walked out of Buckingham Palace as Sir Alan Cobham, Knight of the Order of the British Empire.

The next spin was twenty-three thousand miles around Africa in a Short Singapore flying-boat. These exploits would be popularized by his three books, *My Flight to the Cape, Australia and Back*, and *20,000 Miles in a Flying Boat*.

In the early 1930s he toured Britain with the stunt planes of "Sir Alan Cobham's Air Display" which took the breath away with wing-walks on an Avro 504K and had queues lining up for a flight in his own de Havilland 61, called Youth of Britain, a process which was delayed by the fact that they all wanted the pilot's autograph as a memento. Geoffrey Tyson, the country's best stunt pilot, would show how he could pick up a lady's handkerchief from the ground with a spike attached to the left-hand wing-tip of his Tiger Moth.

The barnstorming days gave way in 1935 to the first experiments with in-flight refuelling, aimed to keep open the air route to India in the event of the gathering storm becoming a full-blown war. A Harrow bomber registration G-AFRL was converted into a fuel tanker and successfully fed Short S30 flying-boats of Imperial Airways in trials above Southampton Water. The hose-link grab attachments were fitted to flying-boats Cabot, Caledonia, Cambria and Caribou.

In the war the system would be used with Wellington bombers as tankers to connect with Hurricanes and Spitfires that were being flown across the entire length of the southern Mediterranean to bases in Egypt. The subsequent post-war story of Cobham's company, Flight Refuelling Limited, is told under its entry and that for Tarrant Rushton Aerodrome.

As for Sir Alan, he went into semi-retirement at Falaise on Bournemouth's West Cliff in the early 1950s. From 1956-67 he was chairman of the Bournemouth Symphony Orchestra which came many times to play on his outsized garden lawn. Lady Gladys died in 1961 and Sir Alan moved to Suffolk in 1970. They are buried in Tarrant Rushton churchyard.

Cobham's Flying Circus — dates of Dorset visits given in the entry for National Aviation Displays.

Cobham plc — Sir Alan Cobham's company, Flight Refuelling Limited, as it was renamed in its founder's honour [1994].

Compton Abbas Airfield — grass leisure aerodrome on top of the Cranborne Chase escarpment, at 810-feet above sea level, on the east side of Spread Eagle Hill (Ordnance Survey map reference SY 890 186). Westerly take-offs, into the prevailing wind, cross the steep slope of the National Trust's Fontmell Down estate and emerge from the spectacular scenery with instant altitude, high above the Blackmore Vale.

Founded by Shaftesbury Flying Club which won planning permission to use the "land for flying light aircraft and erect small blister-type hangar" [22 May 1962]. Detailed permission was then given for the hangar, to house an Auster and two Tiger Moths, but plans for a club-house were rejected [16 November 1962].

The club was later given clearance to use a caravan as its flight control office, and to construct a car-park [8 September 1965].

John Thorne and Ralph Jones took over from the club and were allowed to erect additional buildings [9 July 1968]. Six caravans for members of Dorset Flying Club followed [10 September 1969] and P.W. Lewis was given consent for his own portable hangar. It had the feel of a pre-war aerodrome, particularly after the arrival of the Thames Valley Airsports Parachute Club and the creation of the Spread Eagle Display Team [1970]. The club had a veritable squadron of light aircraft and two Austers were busy towing gliders.

The enterprise had lifted off — sparking its own single-issue protest group — and on the ground John Thorne consolidated the structual presence, by obtaining permission for a restaurant, accommodation, and office block [4 March 1971]. Occasional helicopter arrivals included the Army on manoeuvres. Bill Boot jumped from a Cessna that had taken off from Compton Abbas, whilst over the English side of the Bristol Channel, and claimed to be the first person to parachute across the wide waters of the Severn sea.

Water mains were installed and John Thorne then sold the aerodrome to Ernest Green [1972]. He in turn handed it over to millionaire Alan Curtis of George House (Holdings) Limited [1975]. The new owner brought mains electricity and was given permission to modify and add to the existing airfield buildings [25 July 1976]. A second hangar and aircraft control tower were then authorised [4 August 1976]. North Dorset District Council's file note of planning permission for the oil fuel and oil facilities includes a reference to a "dope store" which is the aviation term for aircraft paint [27 October 1976].

The airfield's postcard manages to say it all, both visually and with its own caption. "Compton Abbas Airfield has the finest views from any airfield in England" — which is true from the ground as well. "Friendly bar, lovely restaurant, flying training, air charters, engineering, aircraft sales, avionics. An aviation centre that caters for everyone."

Including runaway financier Azil Nadir whose escape to northern Cyprus started by posing as a respectable businessman to hire Clive Hughes to fly him to France.

Cordelia — Poole-based British Overseas Airways Corporation Short "Empire" flying-boat, flown to Belfast for a military refit to equip her with four machine guns in each of two Boulton-Paul turrets, in the dorsal and tail, plus armour plating, bomb-racks on the wings, and radar. She became Coastal Command aircraft AX660 and was posted to 119 Squadron for anti-submarine depth charge trials [16 April 1941]. Returned to BOAC's Poole fleet [September 1941] and survived the war, but was scrapped a couple of years later, at Hythe on Southampton Water [6 March 1947].

Corfe Castle crashes — Fairey Swordfish K5985, on a flight along the Channel coast from Gosport, hit trees at Kingston, on the hill to the south of Corfe Castle [18 March 1938].

Messerschmitt Bf.110C (3U+JT) belonging to the 9th Staffel of Zerstörergeschwader 26 made a forced-landing near Corfe Castle after being engaged by the RAF whilst taking part in the German attack on the Westland Aircraft Company at Yeovil [16.00 hours, 7 October 1940].

Gefreiter Bernhardt Demmig, the pilot, survived and was taken prisoner of war, but his Bordfunker, Obergefreiter Josef Bachmann, was killed.

They were shot down by Squadron Leader Michael Robinson, in a Spitfire, who had just taken command of 609 Squadron at RAF Warmwell [4 October 1940]. Flying Officer Richard Brooker joined in the kill, in a Hurricane of 56 Squadron from RAF Boscombe Down.

Hurricane P3984 of 238 Squadron from the newly opened RAF Chilbolton, Hampshire, crashed into the roadside quarry immediately north of Castle Hill [10 October 1940]. Pilot Officer Bob Doe parachuted to safety, on Brownsea Island, after breaking through cloud at 16,000 feet into the sights of Messerschmitt Bf.109s. Both locations are now owned by the National Trust.

Spitfire R7142 of 140 Squadron broke up when trying to pull out of a dive and plunged into heathland near Rempstone [16 December 1941].

Hurricane Z3349, a Mark II fighter of 245 Squadron, force-landed on Furzey Island — in the salt-marshes of Poole Harbour [29 March 1942]. Another Hurricane was lost in the waters off neighbouring Green Island [March 1943].

Two Liberator bombers crashed in the parish of Corfe Castle during the final year of the Second World War. One is said to have flown into a steep hillside above Encombe House, in dense fog [date unknown], and the second fell on Furzey Island in Poole Harbour [July 1944] with the loss of all its American crew.

Coryton — high flyer **Air Chief Marshal Sir Alec Coryton** [born 1895] retired to Two Leas at Langton Matravers. He had been Air Officer Commanding of the Bomber Group at the Air Ministry [1942-43] and Air Commodore of the Third Tactical Air Force, in Bengal and Burma, for South East Asia Command [1944-45]. In Purbeck his pride and joy was the restoration [1948-50] of a 1903 De Dion Bouton which was almost a total wreck. The car was bought in Italy by Daniel Hanbury of Castle Malwood, Lyndhurst, who brought it to England in 1910. Hanbury's daughter, Philippa, married Alec Coryton.

Coventry raid — a massed formation of some 150 German aircraft flew across the Channel on a directional radio beam from the Cherbourg peninsula and crossed the coast at Christchurch and New Milton in the "Moonlight Sonata" attack that devastated the city of Coventry [14-15 November 1940]. The other streams crossed the English coast over Dover and the Wash. The landmark of Coventry Cathedral would be targeted by the pathfinders of Kampfgruppe 100.

Crashes — chronological county list. See parish entries for details of each. This catalogue is comprehensive but no claims are made for completeness. Updatings and additional information will be welcomed by the author and publisher, for incorporation in future editions.

Rolls biplane at Southbourne, Bournemouth [12 July 1910].

Biplane from Talbot Village, Bournemouth [24 April 1916].

Zero Airship at Loders [summer 1917].

Bristol Fighter at Christchurch Road, Bournemouth [22 July 1918].

Supermarine Sea Lion G-EALP off Bournemouth [10 September 1919].

Westland Widgeon at Ensbury Park Racecourse, Bournemouth [6 June 1927].

Blackburn Bluebird at Ensbury Park Racecourse, Bournemouth [6 June 1927].

Peto seaplane with submarine M2 off Portland [26 January 1932].

Blenheim K7056 at Woodsford (Warmwell) Aerodrome [26 November 1937].

Fairey Battle K7594 on the Chesil Beach [11 December 1937].

Westland Wallace K6057 at Holworth, Owermoigne [14 January 1938].

Westland Wallace K6063 at Langton Herring [10 March 1938].

Fairey Swordfish K5985 at Kingston, Corfe Castle [18 March 1938].

Hawker Audax K3086 at Warmwell Aerodrome [12 April 1938].

Hawker Fury K8223 off the Chesil Beach [25 May 1938].

Hawker Fury K8271 on the Chesil Beach [10 December 1938].

Hawker Audax K4396 beside the Chesil Beach [13 March 1939].

Boulton Paul Defiant L6982 at Warmwell Aerodrome [2 April 1940].

Hawker Hind K5544 at Warmwell Aerodrome [3 April 1940].

Fairey Seal K3480 at Langton Herring [22 April 1940].

Boulton Paul Overstrand K8173 off the Chesil Beach [22 April 1940].

Miles Master N7551 at Puddletown [22 April 1940].

Lysander L2057 at Chickerell [23 April 1940].

Hawker Hind K6839 at Warmwell Aerodrome [24 April 1940].

Hawker Hind K5382 at Lytchett Matravers [26 April 1940].

Hawker Hind K5425 at Warmwell Aerodrome [27 April 1940].

Fairey Seal K3480 at Warmwell Aerodrome [7 May 1940].

Junkers Ju.87 off Portland [9 July 1940].

Messerschmitt Bf.110 (2N+EP) at Povington Heath, Tyneham [11 July 1940].

Spitfire L1069 off Portland Bill [11 July 1940].

Spitfire L1095 off Portland [11 July 1940].

Hurricane N2485 off Portland [11 July 1940].

Hurricane P3084 off Portland [12 July 1940].

Hurricane at Little Mayne Farm, West Knighton [13 July 1940].

Dornier Do.17 at Fleet [18 July 1940].

Spitfire on the beach at Studland [18 July 1940].

Spitfire R6634 off Swanage [18 July 1940].

Hurricane P3766 into Lyme Bay [20 July 1940].

Hurricane P3082 into Lyme Bay [20 July 1940].

Spitfire K9880 off Swanage [20 July 1940].

Dornier Do.17 (5F+OM) at Nutford Farm, Pimperne [21 July 1940].

Dornier Do.17 near Weymouth [25 July 1940].

Spitfire K9901 off Portland [25 July 1940].

Spitfire N3023 off Weymouth [27 July 1940].

Spitfire K9894 at Bestwall, Wareham [8 August 1940].

Spitfire R6811 at Spyway Farm, Langton Matravers [8 August 1940].

Junkers Ju.88 (B3+DC) on Portland [11 August 1940].

Messerschmitt Bf.110 near Swanage [11 August 1940].

Messerschmitt Bf.110 off the Dorset coast [11 August 1940].

Hurricane P3585 at Lulworth [11 August 1940].

Hurricane P3598 at Warmwell [11 August 1940].

Hurricane P3222 off Weymouth [11 August 1940].

Hurricane L2057 off Portland [11 August 1940].

Hurricane P3783 off Portland [11 August 1940].

Hurricane P3885 off Portland [11 August 1940].

Hurricane R4092 off Portland [11 August 1940].

Hurricane P2978 off Swanage [11 August 1940].

Hurricane R4094 off the Dorset coast [11 August 1940].

Spitfire R6614 off the Dorset coast [11 August 1940].

Heinkel He.111 (1G+AC) at Sturminster Marshall [12 August 1940].

Hurricane at Bredy Farm, Burton Bradstock [13 August 1940].

Hurricane P3348 off Portland [13 August 1940].

Hurricane P3177 off Portland [13 August 1940].

Junkers Ju.87 at Portesham [13 August 1940].

Junkers Ju.87 (or Messerschmitt Bf.110) at Grimstone, Stratton [13 August 1940].

Messerschmitt Bf.110 (L1+FZ) at Swalland Farm, Kimmeridge [13 August 1940].

Messerschmitt Bf.109 off Weymouth [13 August 1940].

Messerschmitt Bf.109 in Poole Harbour [13 August 1940].

Messerschmitt Bf.109 off the Dorset coast [13 August 1940].

Hurricane at Symondsbury [15 August 1940].

Hurricane at Abbotsbury Swannery [15 August 1940].

Hurricane beside Radipole Lake, Weymouth [15 August 1940].

Hurricane P2872 off Portland [15 August 1940].

Hurricane P3215 off Portland [15 August 1940].

Spitfire R6985 off the Dorset coast [15 August 1940].

Spitfire R6988 at Walsford Road, Bournemouth [15 August 1940].

Messerschmitt Bf.110 (3M+KM) at East Chaldon, Chaldon Herring [25 August 1940].

Messerschmitt Bf.109 into the Chesil Beach at Chickerell [25 August 1940].

Messerschmitt Bf.110 at Tatton House, Chickerell [25 August 1940].

Messerschmitt Bf.110 (3M+KH) at Priory Farm, East Holme [25 August 1940].

Messerschmitt Bf.109 at Tatton Farm, Chickerell [25 August 1940].

Messerschmitt Bf.110 at Creech Barrow Hill, Church Knowle [25 August 1940].

Hurricane V7250 at New Barn, Bradford Peverell [25 August 1940].

Hurricane N2646 at Burton Bradstock {25 August 1940].

Spitfire N3226 at Dorchester [25 August 1940].

Spitfire R6810 off Portland [25 August 1940].

Hurricane N2646 off Portland [25 August 1940].

Hurricane P2766 off Portland [25 August 1940].

Hurricane P3200 off Portland [25 August 1940].

Spitfire R6994 off the Dorset coast [25 August 1940].

Spitfire R6831 off Portland [27 August 1940].

Spitfire N3061 off Weymouth [6 September 1940].

Spitfire at Dorchester [7 September 1940].

Miles Magister P6362 at Emmetts Hill, Worth Matravers [14 September 1940].

Heinkel He.111 off Portland [15 September 1940].

Heinkel He.111 (G1+LR) at Branksome Park, Poole [25 September 1940].

Heinkel He.111 (G1+BH) at Westfield Farm, Studland [25 September 1940].

Spitfire K9882 off Swanage [26 September 1940].

Messerschmitt Bf.110 (S9+JH) at Bussey Stool Farm, Tarrant Gunville [27 September 1940].

Messerschmitt Bf.110 (S9+DU) at The Beeches, Iwerne Minster [27 September 1940].

Messerschmitt Bf.110 (3U+DS) at Gaulter Gap, Kimmeridge [27 September 1940].

Messerschmitt Bf.110 (3U+BD) near Tyneham [27 September 1940].

Messerschmitt Bf.110 at Lulworth Camp [27 September 1940].

Messerschmitt Bf.110 (3U+FT) at Doles Ash Farm, Piddletrenthide [27 September 1940].

Spitfire X4107 at Cheselbourne [27 September 1940].

Messerschmitt Bf.110 (3U+FT) at Salter's Wood, Arne [27 September 1940].

Messerschmitt Bf.109 at Sprigg's Farm, Sydling St Nicholas [30 September 1940].

Hurricane at Oborne Road, Sherborne [30 September 1940].

Spitfire L1702 at Shaftesbury [30 September 1940].

Hurricane N2474 at Shaftesbury [30 September 1940].

Hurricane N2434 at Okeford Fitzpaine [30 September 1940].

Hurricane P2866 at East Knighton, Winfrith Newburgh [30 September 1940].

Hurricane L1764 on Chesil Beach, Abbotsbury [30 September 1940].

Hurricane N2434 at Monkton Wyld, Wootton Fitzpaine [30 September 1940].

Hurricane N2434 at Monkton Wyld, Wootton Fitzpaine [30 September 1940].

Hurricane P2987 at Whitcombe [30 September 1940].

Spitfire L1072 off Portland [30 September 1940].

Hurricane P3655 off Portland [30 September 1940].

Hurricane P3088 off Portland [30 September 1940].

Hurricane P3414 off Weymouth [30 September 1940].

Spitfire L1072 off the Dorset coast [30 September 1940].

Unidentified aeroplane off Hengistbury Head, Bournemouth [1 October 1940].

Hurricane P3599 in Poole Harbour [1 October 1940].

Junkers Ju.88 (9K+5N) at Tapper's Hill, Sydling St Nicholas [7 October 1940].

Messerschmitt Bf.110 (3U+JP) at Brickhills Field, Kingston Russell [7 October 1940].

Messerschmitt Bf.110 at Owermoigne [7 October 1940].

Messerschmitt Bf.110 at Arish Mell Gap, Lulworth [7 October 1940].

Messerschmitt Bf.110 (3U+BT) at Stoborough, Arne [7 October 1940].

Messerschmitt Bf.110 (3U+JT) at Corfe Castle [7 October 1940].

Hurricane V6777 at Meriden Wood, Winterborne Houghton [7 October 1940].

Hurricane at Austral Farm, Alton Pancras [7 October 1940].

Spitfire X4472 at Vale Farm, Sutton Waldron [7 October 1940].

Spitfire N3231 at Netmead, Child Okeford [7 October 1940].

Spitfire N3238 at Watercombe [7 October 1940].

Spitfire N3039 at Shatcombe Farm, Wynford Eagle [7 October 1940].

Hurricane P3984 below Castle Hill, Corfe Castle [10 October 1940].

Hurricane P3421 at Worgret, Wareham [10 October 1940].

Messerschmitt Bf.110 at Bournemouth [15 October 1940].

Spitfire R6607 at Tadnoll Mill, Chaldon Herring [18 October 1940].

Heinkel He.111 (6N+AH) at West Bay, Bridport [6 November 1940].

Junkers Ju.88 at Branksome, Poole [14 November 1940].

Spitfire R6597 near Wareham [28 November 1940].

Spitfire P9427 into Poole Bay [28 November 1940].

Spitfire at Field Grove, Durweston [29 November 1940].

Messerschmitt Bf.109 at Woodyhyde Farm, Worth Matravers [30 November 1940].

German aircraft off Hengistbury Head, Bournemouth [1 December 1940].

Lysander R9015 at Broadwindsor [16 December 1940].

Dornier Do.17 off Portland Bill [4 January 1941].

Hurricane V6758 at Warmwell Aerodrome [4 January 1941].

Whitley T4299 at Connegar Farm, Manston [3 April 1941].

Blenheim T2439 at Frampton [4 April 1941].

Heinkel He.111 on the south Dorset Ridgeway [5 April 1941].

Fairey Battle K9230 off Hengistbury Head, Bournemouth [28 April 1941].

Junkers Ju.88 on Winfrith Heath Decoy Aerodrome, Winfrith Newburgh [4 May 1941].

BOAC flying-boat *Maia* in Poole Harbour [12 May 1941].

Heinkel He.111 (G1+ES) at Patchin's Point, Arne [12 May 1941].

Messerschmitt Bf.109E at Worth Matravers [6 June 1941].

Spitfire P8656 at West Knighton, Winfrith Newburgh [14 July 1941].

Blenheim P4832 off Purbeck coast [17 July 1941].

Spitfire P8516 at Owermoigne [4 August 1941].

Whirlwind P6983 at Hurn Aerodrome [6 August 1941].

Spitfire R6639 at Lulworth [10 September 1941].

Lysander L6860 at Stalbridge [7 October 1941].

Wellington X9677 off St Alban's Head, Worth Matravers [10-11 October 1941].

Hurricane Z4993 at Ridgeway Hill, Weymouth [25 October 1941].

Focke Wulf 190 at Bindon Hill, Lulworth [21 October 1941].

Hurricane at RAF Warmwell [11 November 1941].

Blenheim L9405 off the Chesil Beach [29 November 1941].

Spitfire R7142 at Rempstone, Corfe Castle [16 December 1941].

Wellington X9785 at West Milton, Powerstock [16 December 1941].

Hurricane Z3349 on Furzey Island, Corfe Castle [29 March 1942].

B-17 Flying Fortress at Charity Farm, Lytchett Minster [2 April 1942].

Miles Magister N3980 near Wareham [6 May 1942].

Heinkel He.111 near Shaftesbury [23 May 1942].

Westland Whirlwind P7014 at Warmwell Aerodrome [8 October 1942].

Typhoon R7695 at Glanvilles Wootton [24 October 1942].

Typhoon R8823 at Warmwell Aerodrome [27 October 1942].

Typhoon R8663 at Chilfrome [15 December 1942].

Halifax DT684 in Kingston Lacy Park, Pamphill [24 January 1943].

Westland Whirlwind P6991 at Warmwell Aerodrome [9 February 1943].

Short Stirling R9306 either at Blandford or Creech Barrow Hill, Church Knowle [16 February 1943].

Dornier Do.17 near Beaminster [February 1943].

Hurricane off Green Island, Corfe Castle [March 1943].

Westland Whirlwind P7057 at Warmwell Aerodrome [7 May 1943].

Westland Whirlwind P7059 at Warmwell Aerodrome [22 May 1943].

Seafire MB315 at Caroline Avenue, Christchurch [25 June 1943].

Spitfire EB687 at Hurn Aerodrome [10 July 1943].

Westland Whirlwind P7110 at Warmwell Aerodrome [13 July 1943].

Whitley tug-plane at Hurn Aerodrome [July 1943].

Westland Whirlwind P6981 at Warmwell Aerodrome [1 August 1943].

Westland Whirlwind P7096 at Warmwell [10 September 1943].

Four gliders at East Parley, Hurn [sometime in 1943].

Halifax glider tug-plane [26 January 1944].

Typhoon HHS MN129 at West Knighton [12 March 1944].

Hurricane LD972 near Hurn [21 March 1944].

Halifax JP137 at Moordown, Bournemouth [22 March 1944].

P-47 Thunderbolt at Highcliffe School, Christchurch [30 April 1944].

P-38 Lightning at Cheselbourne [21 May 1944].

Wellington at Christchurch [25 May 1944].

P-47 Thunderbolts in multiple crashes at Foxwood Avenue, Mudeford, Christchurch [29 June 1944].

P-47 Thunderbolt in the Lymington road, Christchurch [2 July 1944].

Mosquito at Alder Road, Poole [23 July 1944].

Liberator on Furzey Island, Corfe Castle [July 1944].

Liberator above Encombe House, Corfe Castle [sometime in 1944].

Martinet at Burton Mere, Burton Bradstock [12 March 1945].

B-17 Flying Fortress 866 at Christchurch Aerodrome [15 July 1945]

Tiger Moth N6658 at Thornford [9 November 1945].

BOAC flying-boat *Hailsham* off Brownsea Island, Poole Harbour [4 March 1946.

Prototype Airspeed Ambassador at Hurn Aerodrome [January 1950].

Airspeed Ambassador G-ALFR at Christchurch Aerodrome [13 November 1950].

Fairey Barracuda off Highcliffe, Christchurch [20 June 1952].

Vampire at Tarrant Rushton Aerodrome [June 1953].

Hunter off the Dorset coast [15 July 1968].

Whirlwind helicopter at Portland [9 October 1968].

Meteor at Blandford [13 February 1969].

Helicopter at Bovington Camp [14 May 1969].

Whirlwind helicopter in Portland Harbour [20 June 1969].

Two Sioux helicopters at Christchurch [23 August 1969].

Canberra into Lyme Bay [1 May 1970].

Phantom off the Dorset coast [13 May 1970].

Wessex helicopter off Portland [20 May 1971].

Sea King helicopter off Portland [13 January 1972].

Wessex helicopter off Portland [16 February 1972].

Balloon Gerard Heineken at Coles Farm, Langton Matravers [25 July 1975].

F-111 at Mapperton, Sturminster Marshall [29 April 1980].

Sea Harrier at Cattistock [21 January 1983].

Pampa 1A-63 at Hurn Aerodrome [31 August 1992].

Montgomery-Benson B8M Autogyro at Stag Gate, Sturminster Marshall [11 December 1993].

Crichel Down Bombing Range — in the parish of Long Crichel, on the chalky foothills of Cranborne Chase, established by the Air Ministry [1939]. Derequisitioned, when civil servants attempted selling the land to a third party — rather than first offering it back to former owner Commander Toby Marten of Crichel House — precipitated the Crichel Down Scandal [1954] which caused the resignation of Conservative Minister of Agriculture Sir Thomas Dugdale. It also nearly ended the political career of Peter Carrington, his Parliamentary Secretary, almost before it had started.

Crook — Spitfire flyer **Pilot Officer David Moore Crook** [1914-44] of 609 Squadron shot down a Junkers Ju.87 "Stuka" off Portland, killing Luftwaffe hero von Dalwigk [9 July 1940]. He claimed a Messerschmitt Bf.110, also over the sea, in another round of Battle of Britain dog-fights [11 August 1940]. A Bf.109 escort fighter, which crashed into the sea, was added to his score on the Luftwaffe's Adlertag (Eagle Day) attack [13 August 1940]. There followed two Bf.109s in a chase across the English Channel, leading Green Section in a line seawards from 23,000 feet over Swanage [30 September 1940]: "I got up to about 500 mph and easily caught mine, gave it a burst and he crashed into the sea. I then chased another and put him in the sea about 25 miles from Cherbourg. It took me a long time to get back to the English coast .... pleased to see the white cliffs."

That was in the morning. In the afternoon he had "a very enjoyable few minutes dog-fighting" and chased a Bf.109 to Weymouth, "and then gave him a good burst. He turned over on to his back and spun into cloud streaming glycol and smoke. I could not claim him a definite as I did not see him actually crash but he certainly never got back to France. This was my best day yet."

Awarded the Distinguished Flying Cross [17 October 1940]. His last action with 609 Squadron would be leading it, also in Spitfire X4165, in the commanding officer's absence [8 November 1940]. He became a flying instructor. Lost over the North Sea whilst flying Spitfire EN662 on a high-level photographic reconnaissance [18 December 1944].

D

DA — code letters of 210 Squadron, operating Catalina flying-boats from RAF Hamworthy [1943].

Dambuster bombs — aircraft designer Barnes Wallis devised the bouncing bomb at Vickers-Armstrongs' Weybridge works, Surrey, and tested its prototypes on The Fleet lagoon in Dorset [December 1942 March 1943]. Wooden dummies and steel spheres were dropped from a height of 60 feet from Wellington BJ895/G which operated on test days from RAF Warmwell.

Several failures were followed by the first successful bounce, though this casing then shattered [January 1943] and then a series of thirteen bounces, east of Langton Hive Point, Langton Matravers [23 January 1943]. The following day the revolutionary bomb not only zipped across the water but jumped a boom which had been prepared to simulate the wall of a dam.

The sheltered and waveless inshore waters, between the Chesil Beach and the mainland shore, replicated conditions on a lake. The final Dorset tests, with the Wellington approaching at 300 miles per hour, achieved distances of around 4,000 feet [5 February 1943].

Fully-weighted steel versions, some of which remained in The Fleet as mooring buoys into recent times, followed a month later [9 March 1943].

Practice runs for the Lancaster bombers of 617 Squadron were transferred to the totally realistic scenario of actual lakes and dams in the Elan Valley of central Wales, where the mountain obstacles matched the hills of the Ruhr.

Operation Chastise would successfully breach the Möhne and Eder dams [16-17 May 1943] in the most audacious and spectacular aerial action of the Second World War; and at the cost of eight of the 19 participating Lancasters, plus 1,294 who were drowned, in the Ruhr, including several hundred Russian prisoners of war.

Dan Air — based its fleet of Hawker-Siddeley 748s at Bournemouth (Hurn) Airport and operated internal passenger flights between British cities [1970s].

Darley — the commander of 609 Squadron at RAF Warmwell throughout the Battle of Britain was **Squadron Leader Horace Stanley "George" Darley** [born 1913]. On one of its busiest days he shot down a Messerschmitt Bf.109 at Chickerell and shared the kill of a Bf.110 over Chaldon Herring [25 August 1940]. His last kill for the squadron was a Dornier Do.17 [25 September 1940].

Posted from Warmwell to become Station Commander of RAF Exeter [4 October 1940] where he heard that he had been awarded the Distinguished Service Order [22 October 1940]. Progressed to command RAF Kuala Lumpur [11 December 1941] and retreated from the Japanese, via Sumatra, to India. His pre-war flying for the RAF had begun in 1932 and he continued in the service until retirement, as a Group Captain [1959].

Dawson — aviation historian **Leslie Dawson**, who lives at Parkstone, was the first to realise that Dorset's uniquely important aerial story had not been told. He wrote what became the lavishly illustrated *Wings over Dorset: Aviation's story in the South* [1983] that then went to an even better illustrated second edition [1989].

My part in its production was to edit the manuscript and catch his infectious enthusiasm. This inspired me to research and contribute text on the *Saladin* balloon, Rhodes-Moorhouse VC, the Peto submarine-aircraft tragedy, and a virtual diary of both the Telecommunications Research Establishment at Worth Matravers and Battle of Britain memories from across the county. I also found a substantial number of photographs and compiled all the captions.

Leslie Dawson was born in Southgate, London. He first flew as an ATC cadet at Hendon, which is now home to the RAF Museum. On moving to Bournemouth he joined 622 Gliding School at Christchurch Aerodrome.

After instructing at the National Gliding Centre, at Lasham, he was appointed chief gliding instructor of the Gliding School, then at Old Sarum in Wiltshire. He was commissioned into the training branch of the RAFVR.

Instructors from the nearby Empire Test Pilot School at Boscombe Down then taught him powered flight, in a Tiger Moth, and he gained a private pilot's licence. He was selected to fly the gliding sequences for the film *Training for Life*.

DB — squadron code of 411 (RCAF) Squadron, briefly flying Mark IXe Spitfires from RAF Warmwell [15 - 23 October 1944].

Deanesley — Spitfire flyer **Flying Officer Edward Christopher "Jumbo" Deanesley** of 152 Squadron from RAF Warmwell delivered the coup de grâce to the Dornier that was the squadron's first kill, but was then shot down in the sea five miles off Portland. He baled out of Spitfire K9901, wounded, but was picked up by a freighter and put ashore at Lyme Regis [25 July 1940].

His next ducking would be into the Channel to the south-east of Poole Bay, twelve miles south of the Needles, when Spitfire K9982 was attacked by a swarm of Messeschmitt Bf.109s [26 September 1940]. This time he was found by an RAF Air-Sea Rescue launch and landed at Swanage.

Transferred to night-fighters at Catterick [23 November 1940], awarded the Distinguished Flying Cross [30 May 1941], and left the RAF at the end of war as Wing Commander [1945].

de Havilland Aircraft Company Limited — owned the Airspeed Limited factory beside Christchurch Aerodrome, Somerford, and eventually absorbed its name [July 1951]. Aside from the Mosquito, Geoffrey de Havilland's famous creation was the prototype Vampire, six of which, in July 1948, became the first jets to cross the Atlantic Ocean.

The jet went into production and at Christchurch a total of 140 were built there, as trainers, followed by Venoms and Sea Venoms, for the Royal Navy.

The factory also produced 23 Airspeed Ambassador airliners. British European Airways used them on their newly-named "Elizabethan" class, on the accession of Queen Elizabeth II [1952].

More successful was the Sea Vixen, with 118 being built at Christchurch, before the company was bought out by Hawker Siddeley which went on to make 22 Mark II versions. These were the last generation of

British aircraft-carrier fighters before the advent of the Sea Harrier.

Production continued at Somerford for a decade but de Havilland then removed the remaining work to its main factory at Chester [1962].

The last Royal Navy Sea Vixen retained its local connection with its sale to Flight Refuelling Limited at Hurn, on its withdrawal from squadron service [1982].

de Virac Lart — veteran flyer **Wing Commander Edward Collis de Virac Lart** [1902-41] of Lyme Regis flew in the 1920s with 60 (Bombing) Squadron in India. He served throughout the Battle of Britain but would be lost the following spring when he failed to return to his base [27 March 1941].

Devitt — experienced pilot **Squadron Leader Peter Devitt** [born 1911] who went to Sherborne School and learnt to fly at West Malling at the age of nineteen [1931], brought 152 (Hyderabad) Squadron from Northumberland to RAF Warmwell [12 July 1940].

He had a remarkably lucky war. His closest call when the return fire from a Heinkel He.111 put shots through his petrol tank. Devitt made a successful forced-landing into the Somerset countryside, at Skew Bridge, Newton St Loe, to the south of Bath [25 September 1940].

Postings followed to the headquarters of No.9 Group [November 1940] and No.14 Group [April 1941]. From there he went to war in the Far East, to No.221 Group in Rangoon, as the Japanese advanced. He commanded the final withdrawal of British forces from Burma, into the Indian state of Assam [8 May 1942].

Promotion followed to Group Captain and Wing Commander. He was to enjoy a long retirement, for upwards of half a century from the end of hostilities.

HMS *Dipper* — the Royal Navy shore-base otherwise known as Henstridge Royal Naval Air Station, which straddled the Dorset-Somerset boundary north of Stalbridge.

Doe — Hurricane flyer **Pilot Officer Bob Doe** of 238 Squadron from RAF Chilbolton, who had recently been awarded the Distinguished Flying Cross, parachuted to safety on Brownsea Island after being wounded by a flight of Messerschmitt Bf.109s as he rose out of dense cloud [10 October 1940]. His fighter crashed into a roadside quarry, now a National Trust cafe and car-park, on the north side of Corfe Castle.

His next emergency over Dorset, caused by his engine cooling system icing up as he flew at night over the sea off Portland Bill, ending with a crash-landing into oil drums beside a snow-covered Warmwell Aerodrome [4 January 1941]. Hurricane V6758 was ripped apart but the pilot fared somewhat better, after fragments of glass had been removed from his eye at Bovington Military Hospital.

He continued his career for the duration of the conflict and into post-war jet fighters, retiring as Wing Commander R. T. F. Doe DSO, DFC and bar.

Dorchester crashes — a British fighter shot down over the county town by Messerschmitt Bf.109s, during a Battle of Britain dog-fight, has been identified as Spitfire N3226 of 602 Squadron [25 August 1940].

Flying Officer Ralph "Bob" Wolton of 152 Squadron from RAF Warmwell lost control of his Spitfire whilst attempting a sudden dive near Dorchester [7 September 1940]. He baled out at 13,000 feet and narrowly missed plunging into the ground beside his fighter, because his parachute did not open until he was little more than a thousand feet above the ground.

Dorset Gliding Club — operates from Eyres Field, beside Puddletown Road at Gallows Hill, between Bere Regis and Wool.

Dorsetshire Aero Club — formed at Dorchester with the Director of Civil Aviation at the Air Ministry, Air Vice-Marshal Sir Sefton Brancker, being the principal guest [23 August 1926]. He had been brought from Hendon, via Worth Matravers, in the Simmonds Spartan biplane operated by the Isle of Purbeck Light Aeroplane Club.

Double Eagle II — the first hot-air balloon to cross the Atlantic, carrying three Americans from Presque Island, Maine, flew high across central Dorset, following the Stour valley from Marnhull to Poole Harbour, via Bere Regis [10.00 to 11.15 hours, 17 August 1978].

There the balloon still had sufficient height to carry on across the English Channel and into mainland Europe, landing south-east of Paris. It had been a distance of 3,150 miles and a flight of 137 hours 6 minutes.

The crewmen were Ben Abruzzo, Maxie Anderson, and Larry Newman.

Douglas — top flyer **William Sholto Douglas** [1893 - 1969] landed the first commercial flight at Ensbury Park Aerodrome, Kinson, near Bournemouth [1919]. By 1940 he would be Deputy Chief of the Air Staff, then Air Officer Commanding-in-Chief of Fighter Command in the midst of the conflicts of 1940-42, finishing the war as Marshal of the Royal Air Force and retiring in 1948 as first Baron Douglas of Kirtleside.

DP — squadron code of 193 (Fellowship of the Bellows) Squadron, flying rocket-firing Typhoons on cross-Channel missions from RAF Hurn [3-11 July 1944].

Drummond-Hay — young Spitfire flyer **Pilot Officer Peter Drummond-Hay** of 609 Squadron was lost with his fighter, over the sea off Portland, in one of the first Battle of Britain dog-fights [9 July 1940].

DU —squadron code of the Czech 312 Squadron, flying Spitfires on three postings to RAF Warmwell [1942 - 43].

Dundas — Spitfire flyer **Flying Officer John Charles Dundas** [1916-1940] of 609 Squadron at RAF Warmwell claimed a Messerschmitt Bf.110 but his kill managed to limp back to France [13 July 1940]. His first confirmed kill was another Bf.110, which crashed near Swanage [11 August 1940]. A Junkers Ju.87 "Stuka" gunner ruptured Dundas's oil system, stopping the Spitfire's propeller, in the Luftwaffe's Adlertag (Eagle Day) attack [13 August 1940]. He successfully glided the fighter from Portland to a perfect forced-landing at Warmwell Aerodrome.

Similarly the following month, with shell splinters in his leg, after the probable kill of one of the Messerschmitt Bf.110 fighter-bombers involved in the attack on the Westland Aircraft factory [7 October 1940]. Belching smoke and white ethylene glycol coolant, the German aircraft was last seen crossing the coast at Weymouth, and presumed to have crashed in the sea. Its parting shot hit Spitfire R6915 and Dundas's leg; the former would be repaired as it is the fighter that now hangs from the ceiling in the main hall of the Imperial War Museum, and was also flown by Noel le Chevalier Agazarian.

John Dundas was back in the air the next day, promoted Flight-Lieutenant, and awarded the Distinguished Flying Cross [10 October 1940].

His next kill, at 18,000 feet as he swept westwards after soaring alone above Christchurch, was a Bf.110, which crashed on the edge of Bournemouth [15 October 1940]. He was leading Blue Flight at the time, and it was 609 Squadron's ninety-ninth accepted claim.

A "practice flight" over Poole Bay turned into an outing to France, with an apparent kill at the end, as he followed a Junkers Ju.88 — which had been over Southampton — to its base on the Cherbourg peninsula, where he left it lurching out of control with flames shooting from the port engine [27 November 1940].

"I've finished an Me.109 - whoopee!" These would be the last words received by radio from John Dundas in Spitfire X4586, over the sea off the Isle of Wight [28 November 1940]. It might have been the Messerschmitt Bf.109E of Major Helmut Wick, leading Jagdgeschwader 2, who had 57 white kills-bars painted on his rudder. The Luftwaffe ace and Dundas disappeared the same day. Neither body was recovered.

Durweston crash — Spitfire R6907 and Pilot Officer John Woodward Allen of 152 Squadron from RAF Warmwell dived into a wood at Field Grove, near Travellers' Rest, Durweston [29 November 1940]. It was thought that he fainted through loss of oxygen. This is one of the few Second World War crash sites to be marked by a plaque, initially on the trunk of a tree killed by the impact, later replaced by a granite memorial [1978].

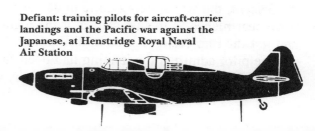

Defiant: training pilots for aircraft-carrier landings and the Pacific war against the Japanese, at Henstridge Royal Naval Air Station

E

East Holme crash — at Priory Farm, of Messerschmitt Bf.110 (3M+KH) belonging to the 1st Staffel of II Gruppe, Zerstörergeschwader 2, in one of Dorset's busiest days during the Battle of Britain [25 August 1940]. The two crew parachuted into captivity.

Edge — Spitfire pilot **Flying Officer Alexander Rothwell Edge** [1908-85] successfully crash-landed on the Studland beach minefield after a Battle of Britain dog-fight [18 July 1940]. He was rescued from the sea, by the Royal Navy.

Posted to Training Command [2 August 1940] he was promoted to Squadron Leader.

Edward, Prince of Wales, forced down at Swanage — Purbeck's least expected royal visit took place at about 13.15 hours in the afternoon, on 12 July 1933 when the Prince of Wales [1894-1972, briefly King Edward VIII] landed in a cornfield near Godlingston Farm. The Channel coast was being lashed by a gale and the Prince, after flying over Bournemouth, was heading for Weymouth, to open the harbour and pier reconstruction.

Visibility was becoming poor and the plane increasingly bumped by the wind. Prince Edward asked the pilot to land in a field. He took his position from the buildings of Swanage Brick and Tile Company, using the chimney stack as a landmark and circling it a couple of times as he descended.

"We thought at first he was going to knock it off," said works director B.P. Codling, referring to the chimney, "but the plane came down nicely in a little wheatfield on the other side of the road from here, on land owned by the Bankes Estate (now National Trust property). The pilot pulled her up by the side of a rick. Afterwards we could find no trace of its descent, the wheat being quite undamaged. Several of our tilers who were near rushed to the assistance of the plane, having seen it in the air, and got the impression it was in difficulties."

The pilot admitted the landing had been far from easy. As for Prince Edward, he was given a lift to Weymouth by Captain F.R. Bacon of the brickworks. Britain's most fashionable dapper-dresser arrived looking none too spruce, the Bournemouth Daily Echo reported; "His hair was very ruffled and his suede shoes were clogged with mud. His trouser ends were bespattered with mud."

EE — code letters of 296 Squadron, flying Halifax tug-planes from RAF Hurn [1943].

8A — squadron code of 298 Squadron, flying Halifax tug-planes from RAF Tarrant Rushton [1943-44].

8E — squadron code of 295 Squadron, flying Halifax tug-planes for airborne forces, from RAF Hurn [1943-44].

EL — squadron code of 181 Squadron, flying rocket-firing Typhoons on cross-Channel missions from RAF Hurn [1 April - 20 June 1944].

Emergency Dispersal Point — of RAF Strike Command, for Valiant and Victor bombers carrying nuclear weapons during times of Cold War tension, was established at Tarrant Rushton [1958]. One of a chain of such airfields, intended to proliferate the number of prime targets and increase the chances of a military survival in the event of a Russian first-strike, this took pressure off the vulnerable front-line East Anglian bases.

The principal users of Tarrant Rushton were Valiants of 148 Squadron from RAF Marham, Norfolk, until their early demise from metal fatigue and the consequent disbandment of the unit [1965].

Ensbury Park Aerodrome and Racecourse — in the old Dorset parish of Kinson, now under the houses of Leybourne Avenue and adjoining suburban streets in Northbourne, Bournemouth (Ordnance Survey map reference SZ 080 955). Created by Bournemouth Aviation Company, for the training of Royal Flying Corps pilots in the Great War [1917]. Their activities moved here from Talbot Village Aerodrome. Accidents were inevitable and included that which killed Major John Lockock [22 July 1918].

William Sholto Douglas made the first scheduled commercial peacetime flight from Ensbury Park [6 June 1919], in an ex-military

Handley Page 0-400, D8350 of Handley Page Transport Limited, for whom he was the chief pilot. The aircraft was repainted with the civilian identification G-EAAE. Sholto Douglas would become Air Officer Commanding-in-Chief of Fighter Command in the Battle of Britain, and Marshal of the Royal Air Force.

Most post-war flying was for fun, culminating with the Killjoy Stakes which were to bring about their own downfall when Westland Widgeon G-EBPW collided with a Blackburn Bluebird, killing Westland's test pilot, Major Laurence Openshaw [6 June 1927]. A series of accidents prompted official intervention to end the heady days of low-level competitive flights.

Transferred from the county of Dorset to Hampshire and the expanding countryside borough of Bournemouth [1930]. Soon after that it became a housing estate, crossed by Leybourne Avenue and Saxonhurst Road [1932].

E7 — squadron code of 570 Squadron, flying Albemarle and Stirling tug-planes for airborne forces from Hurn and Tarrant Rushton [1944].

Euro Direct Airlines — operated from Bournemouth (Hurn) Airport with four flights a day on its service to Amsterdam [winter 1994], which had become Bournemouth's most popular route. A 56-seat, British-built ATP aircraft was introduced for most of the services to Holland and Paris.

An earlier evening flight was also scheduled for the Brussels route [leaving 18.15 hours], which is a half-hour flight time [18.45 arrival].

For the first time, travellers to Paris were offered what was being termed "a genuine day-return in both directions". Flights were leaving Bournemouth at 07.20, 14.35 and 18.40 hours, with return departures from Charles de Gaulle Airport at 06.55, 10.25 and 17.25 hours.

The all-day shuttle between Bournemouth to Exeter, with up to seven flights a day between the two towns, continued to operate throughout the year. The daily service from Bournemouth to Manchester was increased from once a day to twice a day, giving it day-return status with a morning and evening flight in both directions.

Dublin continued to be well covered, with three flights each weekday and one on Sunday, and Aberdeen had a single weekday flight [07.45 departure for 13.10 arrival].

Overseas, Berne received an evening flight [16.05 departure for 20.40 arrival] daily except for Saturday.

Evans — Halifax flyer **Sergeant Pilot Dennis Evans** [1923-44] was killed when his heavily loaded aircraft stalled shortly after take-off from RAF Hurn, bound for North Africa, and crashed on the Bournemouth suburb of Moordown [22 March 1944]. He was from Middlesex.

Express Air Services — operated from Bournemouth (Hurn) Airport [1970s].

Eyres Field — beside Puddletown Road at Gallows Hill, between Bere Regis and Wool, is the airfield of Dorset Gliding Club (Ordnance Survey map reference SY 845 903).

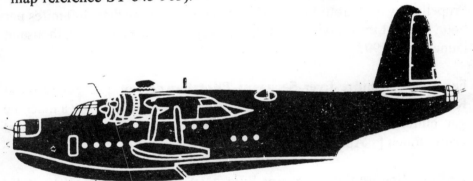

Empire flying-boat: commonest big bird of Poole Harbour, maintaining essential wartime passenger services to Africa and British India, joined by the Short Sunderland service version for Coastal Command attacks on U-boats, from RAF Hamworthy

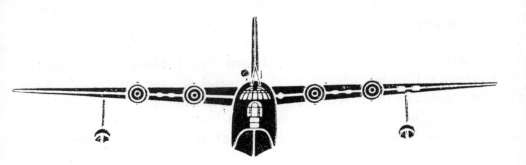

F

Falaise — a mansion built in an acre of clifftop at 13 West Overcliff Drive, Bournemouth [1913] was the home of pioneer aviator Sir Alan Cobham [1894-1973]. This red-brick house has a 40 feet lounge with Adam-style fireplaces and a variety of rooms for the purpose of facilitating those home comforts, such as a flower arranging room. The two floors above have eleven bedrooms with the top line of dormer windows looking out across the Purbeck Hills and the English Channel.

Falconet — pilotless Advanced Subsonic Aerial Target developed for the Ministry of Defence by Flight Refuelling Limited of Wimborne [1982]. Propelled by a Microturbo TJA-24 jet engine, at more than 400 miles per hour, and put into service use [1986]. Now well in excess of a thousand launchings [1995].

Fawcett — Spitfire flyer **Sergeant Pilot Fawcett** of 152 Squadron at RAF Warmwell was killed by the Luftwaffe on the ground, by a machine gun bullet from one of three Heinkel He.111 surprise raiders, as he sat eating lunch [1 April 1941].

Feary — Spitfire flyer **Sergeant Pilot Alan Norman Feary** [1912-1940] of 609 Squadron from RAF Warmwell was killed in action against the Luftwaffe [7 October 1940]. He was hit by Messerschmitt Bf.109s over Weymouth. Though he baled out from Spitfire N3238, as it crashed at Watercombe Farm, he was too low for his parachute to open. "ONE OF THE FEW", his gravestone reads, in the RAF plot at Warmwell churchyard.

Fisher — stunt-flyer **Francis Colebourne "Bud" Fisher** was the pioneer aviator at Christchurch [1931-33]. He was flashy and flamboyant, taking passengers up in his Avro 504K biplane, and operated from a field near the town before the creation of Christchurch Aerodrome [1935]. His activities attracted a total of 160 aircraft, including a memorable visit from Sir Alan Cobham's Flying Circus [30 April 1933].

Financially, however, he was less stable, and lived in a tent beside his aeroplane. Despite the hand-to-mouth existence he found the means to organise the short-lived Bournemouth Flying Club. He answered his country's call at the beginning of the Second World War and enlisted in the RAF as a Flying Officer [23 September 1939] and would retire as Squadron Leader. His last known occupation was as a gentleman model, for dinner jackets and lounge suits.

5V — squadron code of 439 (Royal Canadian Air Force) Squadron flying Mark IV Hurricanes from RAF Hurn [18 March - 2 April 1944] and returning with rocket-firing Typhoons for cross-Channel missions [19 April - 11 May and 20 May - 27 June 1944].

FJ — squadron code of 164 (Argentine-British) Squadron, flying rocket-firing Typhoons on cross-Channel missions from RAF Hurn [26 June - 17 July 1944].

Fleet crash — of a Dornier Do.17 bomber, close to the church, being the second German aircraft to be brought down in Dorset during the Battle of Britain [18 July 1940].

Fleet Requirements Unit — provided target-towing and "enemy attacks" for the Fleet Air Arm and its aircraft-carriers in the English Channel and South-Western Approaches, operating from Bournemouth (Hurn) Airport [1952]. As well as naval fighters, provided by Airwork Services, the unit progressed from Mosquitoes through a series of ex-RAF jet fighters, such as the Meteor and Hunter, and Canberra bombers painted in distinctive black and yellow stripes. Redeployed to the Royal Naval Air Station at Yeovilton [1972].

Flight Refuelling Limited — the need for a "Petrol Supply Co Ltd" of the skies was predicted in a *Punch* cartoon [1909], carried out by "Flying Tankerman" Wesley May over Long Beach, California [12 November 1921], and shown to be a practical reality with the supply line from a

Vickers Virginia tanker feeding a Westland Wapiti at Hendon Air Pageant [1931]. Turning it into a commercial proposition was jinxed by misfortune. Four died aboard Handley Page W10 tanker G-EBMM as it disintegrated after refuelling Sir Alan Cobham's Courier G-ABXN which was attempting an endurance flight to Karachi [22 September 1934].

Undaunted, he founded his own company, Flight Refuelling Limited, with its name proclaiming that the idea could be made to work [29 October 1934]. The Air Ministry provided two retired Vickers Virginias, J7711 and K2668, which fed each other via a system powered by a primitive windmill, to achieve pumping pressure. This was no more effective than relying on gravity.

Progress was illusory until the Air Ministry loaned an Armstrong Whitworth 23 (K3585) and Handley Page 51 (J9833) and the "Wing Tip" method of hose attachment was used [1937]. Empire flying-boat G-ADUV *Cambria* took off from Short Brothers' factory at Rochester, on the Medway, and was refuelled over Felixstowe by K3585 [1938].

This was repeated numerous times and with other aircraft, such as Harrow tanker G-AFRL fuelling G-AFCU *Cabot* over the ocean terminal at Southampton Docks [1939] in an audacious propaganda picture to show that aviation could provide the liners of the future. Hose nozzles and couplings evolved into integrated fittings.

Then came war which curtailed the peacetime opportunities and initially the situation was too defensive to offer much scope for long-range visionaries. Instead Cobham's company was diverted into producing de-icing systems and Sir Alan was asked by Lord Beaverbrook, the mercurial Minister of Aircraft Production, for help in finding new airfields.

Fears that Malta might fall to the Italians revived thoughts of mid-air refuelling, and the practicalities of towing fighters eastwards across the Mediterranean behind bombers fitted out as tankers. A Wellington was chosen for the towed-fighter tests — leading and feeding a Hurricane — and Cobham's 16-year-old son, Michael, was among the bomber's crews. Group Captain William Proctor Wilson flew the fighter and had several near-death experiences in which the over-stretched tow rope was released with only moments to spare.

Post-war the opportunities mushroomed. War's real gift to Flight Refuelling Limited was six surplus Lancaster bombers that were converted into bulk-fuel tankers. Based in Worcestershire, they came south to rendezvous with the British South American Airways fleet, over the English Channel.

Sir Alan Cobham and BSAA chairman Air Vice Marshal Donald "Pathfinder" Bennett took G-AHJV over the mid-Atlantic and refuelled in mid-ocean, enabling them to make the first non-stop flight to Bermuda [28 May 1947].

Cobham's fleet now needed its own sizeable aerodrome and this he found between Blandford and Badbury Rings, with a tenancy of redundant RAF Tarrant Rushton [May 1947].

The Russians then blocked land access to the western sectors of Berlin, suddenly causing an international need for airborne bulk-fuel tankers. Flight Refuelling Limited had 12 of them, plus the expertise necessary to break the blockade, and was the petroleum arm of the Berlin Airlift [1948-49].

The United States Air Force was now at the leading edge of aerial fuelling capability, and proved it by sending Boeing B-50A *Lucky Lady II* on a non-stop flight around the world [26 February - 2 March 1949]. Flight Refuelling Limited countered by developing more sophisticated probe and drogue technology, which was demonstrated at Tarrant Rushton to a visiting American delegation.

Air Chief Marshal Sir Alec Coryton, who would soon retire to Langton Matravers, took the British cause under his wing and provided Avro Lincoln tanker RA657 and Meteor fighter VZ389 for a series of trials.

It hardly compared with the Americans going once round the globe, but Lancaster G-33-2, flown by Tom Marks, enabled Pat Hornidge's Meteor to stay in the sky, above the English Channel, for an endurance flight of 12 hours 3 minutes [7 August 1949]. Hornidge then took the RAF's Lincoln across the Atlantic to show how the Brits were doing it.

USAF B-29 tanker YKB-29T showed that for their part the Americans did things bigger — proving it from Tarrant Rushton with a simultaneous sky-link from wing tips and tail to three British Meteors.

Canberra B2 bomber WH734 was delivered to Tarrant Rushton for conversion to Britain's first jet tanker, its arrival coinciding with the coronation and, appropriately, the climbing of Everest [May 1953].

WH734, intended for trials in refuelling Britain's V-bomber force, remained seconded to Flight Refuelling until after the Falklands War. The first of the new bombers, the Valiant, also provided conversions to tankers, as would the Victors when onset of metal fatigue caused their premature retirement.

Valiant tankers of 214 Squadron enabled Wing Commander Michael Beetham to take a delta-wing Vulcan bomber of 617 "Dambusters" Squadron non-stop from RAF Scampton to Sydney in 20 hours 3 minutes; an average speed of 573 miles per hour [1961]. Cobham's technology had enabled them to improve upon Sir Alan's pre-war record-breaking flight over the same course, which had taken 36 days.

Flight Refuelling had its main problems on the ground. It was preparing to relinquish its lease on Tarrant Rushton, upon which the control tower would be demolished [1981], and would have to move its aircraft to Hurn. It had already built an extensive factory midway between the two airfields, beside the River Stour east of Wimborne.

The Cold War continued but a lesser dispute would put technology to the test.

In the event we never did bomb Russia, notwithstanding Kenny Everett's exhortation to Young Conservatives, and the great British example of aerial refuelling would occur during the Falklands War [1982]. The Victor tankers of 55 Squadron and 57 Squadron flew more than 3,000 hours, carrying near 5,500 tonnes of fuel, in 600 refuelling link-ups.

Eleven of the Victors were needed for aerial sorties with Vulcan "Black Buck 1" which carried out the furthest and longest bombing raid in history — to drop 21 1,000-lb high explosive bombs on or beside Port Stanley airfield. Five more refuelling sorties were needed for the bomber, now much lighter, on its way back to Ascension Island. The flight totalled 7,800 miles and was the only time a V-bomber would be used in anger.

Those Victor tankers outlived the Vulcan bombers and would join Chinook fuel-carrying helicopters of 7 Squadron in supplying air and ground needs of allied forces in the Gulf War [1990]. This vindicated the decision of the US Navy to adopt a probe and drogue system. Whatever the nationality, if the aircraft had a probe then the RAF was able to fuel it in the air — and did so, with a fleet that included VC.10 and Lockheed Tristar tankers as well as the faithful Victors.

Target towing became big business, initially with a fleet of Canberra T.22 bombers, and developed into "Threat Simulation" and "Electronic Warfare", these tasks then being carried out by Falcon 20s, bought from Federal Express.

Flight Refuelling as a company and a concept deserves and has received its own book, by Colin Cruddas, which is entitled *In Cobhams'* (sic) *Company* and published by Cobham plc, the new operating name for Flight Refuelling Limited [1994]. My "sic" is for its aberrant apostrophe. Though it passed to son Michael Cobham, this was Sir Alan's company, and writing of "Cobhams" makes for a clumsy plural, in the literary rather than the aviation sense.

Flying-boats — operated from Poole Harbour, which became the main base for Imperial Airways [August 1939] at the time it was being transformed into the British Overseas Airways Corporation [1 January 1940]. The fleet of Short C-class "Empire" flying-boats were evacuated to Poole from Southampton Water.

Military flying-boats followed, to RAF Hamworthy, and flew anti-submarine patrols for Coastal Command.

FM — squadron code of 257 (Burma) Squadron, flying Mark Ib Typhoons from RAF Warmwell [8 January - 12 August 1943; 17 September 1943 - 20 January 1944] and returning to take their rocket-firing Typhoons on cross-Channel missions from RAF Hurn [2-8 July 1944].

Foss — Bridport war author **Sergeant Pilot Ronald Foss** had gone missing on a Coastal Command flight over the Bay of Biscay [1943]. First to know was his wife who served in the operations room at the same air station. In the event Foss survived and would be picked up from the sea a week later.

He had enough experiences for a book and proceeded to write *In the Drink*, which was followed by *Three of us Live*, and *Famous War Stories*.

Frampton crash — of Blenheim bomber T2439 of 101 Squadron en route back to RAF West Raynham, Norfolk, after a raid on the port of Brest [4 April 1941]. The three crewmen, Sergeants P.T. Burrows, G.B.H. Birdsell and H.R. Perry, were killed instantaneously as the aeroplane exploded on hitting the ground. They had been trying to chart a course to RAF Boscombe Down which is 45 miles to the north-east.

F3 — squadron code of 438 (RCAF Wild Cat) Squadron, flying Mark IV Hurricanes from RAF Hurn [18 March - 3 April 1944] and returning with rocket-firing Typhoons for cross-Channel missions [19 April - 27 June 1944].

Flamingo: last flight to Paris, secretly
carrying Prime Minister Winston Churchill
from RAF Warmwell, on the eve of the fall of France

Liberator: Premier Churchill's personal transport
for the second half of World War Two was based
at RAF Hurn

G

Gee Chain navigation system — one of ten transmitting stations, nationally, including RAF Worth Matravers in Dorset [1942-70]. Operating in pairs, these provided accurately timed radio pulses for British aircrew, who used the signals to plot their aircraft's position by intersecting hyperbolic lines on a pre-printed lattice chart. The system "revolutionised the effectiveness of RAF bombing raids" with "targets being found and bombed as never before". The first to use it operationally was a Wellington of 115 Squadron from RAF Watton, Norfolk, captained by Pilot Officer Jack Foster.

The stations continued in operation through the Cold War, but by the late 1960s the Ministry of Defence considered that other ground-based navigation aids and airborne systems had made Gee obsolete, causing the abandonment of the ten stations and the demolition of their tall aerials.

Gill — sculptor **Eric Gill** [1882-1940], who created the Briantspuddle war memorial, underwent a notionally aeronautic interlude in Dorset.

In September 1918, Gill was conscripted into the Royal Air Force. Sans beard, he was sent to the Mechanical Transport Camp, at Blandford Camp, to be a driver.

Describing it as "an utterly unfriendly and unchristian place" he found "a terrible lot of waiting around" as the war wound down and its last decimations came from disease rather than conflict. Gill's brother, Kenneth, was "a life just thrown away" in an air crash in France, but at Blandford Eric was more fortunate in being hospitalised with influenza and being able to walk away from the problem. The Royal Air Force Camp was particularly hard hit by the pandemic.

Twenty-nine of the victims died; the majority of them young men from the Recruits Wing. Gill was discharged in November 1918 and never again went beardless. "Nation shall speak peace unto nation," he would engrave in his own typographical lettering on the wall of Broadcasting House. He designed the classic sans-serif typeface that carries his name.

GJX — radio pundit code for the Poole Harbour flying-boat base of British Overseas Airways Corporation [1939-48]. The Morse code letters interrupted a continuous tone, at 30 second intervals, and were broadcast from a mobile aerial during wartime and then, in peacetime, directly from the Marine Terminal at Salterns Pier.

Glanvilles Wootton crash — Hawker Typhoon R7695 of 266 Squadron, from RAF Warmwell, broke-up in mid air as it flew over the village [24 October 1942].

Goodman — "One of the Few" **Wing Commander Geoffrey Goodman** [1916-76] is buried in Witchampton churchyard. He was a pre-war pilot who joined the Royal Air Force and was posted to the re-formed 85 Squadron at Debden [1 June 1938]. Flew with them to France, in a Hurricane, on the outbreak of war. Returned injured and later re-joined the squadron at RAF Martlesham Heath [July 1940].

Claimed a Messerschmitt Bf.110 destroyed [30 August 1940] and a Bf.109 fighter [1 September 1940]. Transferred to 29 Squadron at RAF West Malling [November 1942], where his claims were one Dornier Do.217 damaged and a second destroyed. Awarded the Distinguished Flying Cross.

Promoted Flight-Lieutenant and posted to RAF Middle Wallop to command 151 Squadron [October 1943], where in a Mosquito XII night-fighter he accounted for eight enemy aircraft in just two months. Remained with the service after the war, moving to its Engineer Branch, and retiring as a Wing Commander [1969].

Gowers — Hurricane pilot **Flying Officer Arthur Vincent Gowers** [1913-43] from Boscombe, Bournemouth, flew with 85 Squadron in France from the beginning of the Second World War until its withdrawal for home defence [22 May 1940].

In the Battle of Britain he accounted for a Messerschmitt Bf.110 one day and a Bf.109 the next [30-31 August 1940]. The following day, however, he was shot down in V7343 over Oxted, Surrey, and baled out with severe burns. Awarded the Distinguished Flying Cross and promoted

Flight-Lieutenant, he was later posted to RAF Church Fenton to form the new 183 Squadron [1 November 1942], which he commanded until he was killed [24 October 1943].

Gray — fire hero **Group Captain John Astley Gray** DFC [born 1899] from Maiden Newton was awarded the George Medal [September 1941] for "displaying great bravery in the most appalling circumstances".

Acting Squadron Leader Joseph Aiden MacCarthy, an RAF doctor, received the same award for his part in the incident, when an aeroplane landed at night without its undercarriage and careered into a bomb dump. Gray and MacCarthy ignored the flames and bursting ammunition as they tried to save the crew, until they were overcome by fumes.

Gray had won his Distinguished Flying Cross in the Great War, remained in the RAF as a Flight Lieutenant in the 1920s, and was promoted Wing Commander in 1938. He would rise to be an Air Vice-Marshal [1944] and served with Transport Command after the war.

Guba [G-AGBJ] — the first of the long-range American-built Consolidated Catalina flying-boats to land on the water-runways of Poole Harbour [1 February 1941] for use on the BOAC service to Lisbon in neutral Portugal. The roar of her Pratt and Whitney Twin Wasp engines contrasted with the familiar and somewhat gentler sound of the Bristol Pegasus 9-cylinder radial engines of Short "Empire" flying-boats.

Guest — flyer and politician **Captain the Right Honourable Frederick Edward "Freddie" Guest** [1875-1937] was the third son of the first Baron Wimborne. He was private secretary to cousin Winston Churchill. Guest's first election to Parliament, for East Dorset constituency in 1910, was declared void because his mother, Lady Wimborne, of Canford House, Canford Magna, Poole, had bought votes. Undaunted, she set about his re-election in the third contest that year.

He would become Lloyd George's Chief Whip [1917] and Secretary of State for Air [1921-22]. He established Moortown as his private airfield for the Canford estate and became a Squadron Leader in the Auxiliary Air Force, flying an Avro DH9a bomber with 600 Squadron.

H

Hamel — pioneer aviator **Gustav Hamel** [1861-1922] visited Meyrick Park, Bournemouth, [9-12 April 1914] to give breathtaking displays with his monoplane, taking up passengers ranging from Prince Maurice of Battenberg to the lucky holder of the winning raffle ticket.

As he looped the loop and performed other stunts, including a record 21 loops in a single spiral descent, the world entered the summer that would turn to war, and see the English members of the Battenberg family renouncing their titles in favour of the surname Mountbatten.

Hailsham — BOAC Sunderland flying-boat of the *Hythe* class [named January 1946] which came to grief in Poole Harbour on returning to England from Singapore [4 March 1946]. The runway "Trots" were shrouded in fog and she lurched off-course into the shallows beside Brownsea Island, becoming a sodden hulk that was later refloated and towed away for scrap.

Hamilton — BOAC flying-boat, outward bound from Hythe on Southampton Water to Poole Harbour to pick-up passengers for a flight to Singapore [11 November 1947]. Disorientated, in fog, she somehow managed to fly due south, into the 702-feet slope of Brighstone Down, in the centre of the Isle of Wight.

Three of the four crew escaped with their lives, thanks to the cushioning effect of post-war afforestation which had clad the hillside with young pine trees.

RAF Hamworthy — established for the Sunderland flying-boats of Coastal Command, on anti-submarine duties in the English Channel, South-Western Approaches, and into the Bay of Biscay [August 1942]. Squadron-Leader R.C. Lovelock brought 461 (Royal Australian Air Force) Squadron, with nine Sunderlands, from Mount Batten, Plymouth [31 August 1942].

Squadron headquarters were requisitioned on the north-east shore of Poole Harbour, in the Harbour Yatcht Club buildings at Lilliput. This base was initially called RAF Poole but this changed to RAF Hamworthy a week later.

The Australians operated from Hamworthy during the winter and left in the spring for Pembroke Dock, South Wales [21 April 1943].

They were replaced by 210 Squadron, flying military Catalina flying-boats [May - December 1943]. They were able to fly longer range missions, deep into the Atlantic, with airborne radar causing a decisive kill-rate of German U-boats and turning the tide in the Battle of the Atlantic.

By the end of the year the Catalinas had been withdrawn, to enable the Hamworthy slipway and other facilities to be used for training exercises to load landing craft with tanks and other vehicles, in preparation for the invasion of Europe.

Military Sunderland flying-boats returned to RAF Hamworthy for transport duties, rather than attacking U-boats [13 January 1944]. They were operated by 44 Group Transport Command and carried aircrew and other personnel to Karachi, on the route via Gibraltar, Tunis, and Cairo, for the campaign against the Japanese in India and Burma.

The base was hurriedly closed in the hectic run-up to D-Day when its facilities and slipways were needed for the gathering armada of invasion landing craft [March 1944].

HE — squadron code of 263 Squadron, flying rocket-firing Typhoons on cross-Channel missions from RAF Hurn [10-23 July 1944].

Hébert — French flyer **Jean Hébert**, with Denys Boudard, stole a Luftwaffe Bucker Jungmann biplane from an airfield near Caen and flew to Christchurch Aerodrome [29 April 1941]. They joined the Free French Forces. Hébert would be lost over the sea in 1943.

Henstridge Royal Naval Air Station — operated as shore-base HMS *Dipper*, on the Somerset border at Stalbridge (Ordnance Survey map reference ST 750 205). Effectively a satellite to Yeovilton Royal Naval Air Station.

Built on 355 acres of Blackmore Vale pastures and meadows, north-east of Stalbridge and east of Henstridge Marsh [August 1941] with 18 acres being added at Gibbs Marsh Farm, for an Aircraft Rectification Hangar, as the airfield neared completion [1943].

Commissioned as *HMS Dipper* and taken over by No.2 Naval Air Fighter School from Yeovilton. Its flying unit, operating Seafire 1Bs, was 761 (Fleet Air Arm) Squadron. Additional accommodation was found in Fifehead Magdalen village.

Deck-landing practising would be its speciality. Indeed it had a dummy deck — the five runways incorporated an area of concrete laid out like the deck of an aircraft-carrier with arrester wires for added realism.

The 42 Spitfires of No.3 Naval Fighter Wing, from Lee on Solent, used Henstridge during the preparations for D-Day [March 1944].

Subsequently, during the hectic training for the Pacific War, Henstridge was the only Naval Fighter School equipped with Seafires [October 1944].

Seafire squadrons were trained there prior to transfer to aircraft-carriers, such as 887 and 894 (Fleet Air Arm) Squadrons which comprised No.24 Royal Navy Fighter Wing which flew from HMS *Indefatigable* in the Pacific theatre [from December 1944].

She became the first British carrier to be hit by a Japanese kamikaze pilot [1 April 1945]. Among the pilots of 887 Squadron was Sub-Lieutenant R. Lygo, who would retire as Admiral Sir Raymond Lygo.

The Naval School of Army Co-Operation also used Henstridge until its removal to Northern Ireland [August 1945]. and the end of intensive training with the disbanding of 761 Squadron after the war [March 1946].

Henstridge became a satellite airfield for Yeovilton though its aircraft-carrier runway would be brushed off for use in the Korean War period [1949-51], particularly by 767 (Fleet Air Arm) Squadron and the training of deck landing control officers. With the departure of 767 Squadron [September 1952] the airfield was effectively inactive.

Cold War tensions revived its fortunes [1954] and much of the deck landing practice now took place at night — to a crescendo of local opposition. This did much to bring about the final military withdrawal [June 1957].

Civilian activities centred on the exploits and ambitions of one man, former Westland's test-pilot Alan Bristow. His Air Whaling Limited, for Antarctic whale spotting [1953-54] was followed by Bristow Helicopters Limited [1954-68]. Four Widgeons were leased to Shell for oil exploration in the Persian Gulf but the enterprise became almost too successful for Henstridge, being moved to Redhill [1958] where it was nearer Bristow's Cranleigh home.

The Admiralty sold-off the land and hangars. For a time it seemed likely that Henstridge would have the aerials for the BBC World Service [1980] but that plan aroused vociferous protests. Instead Aly Aviation returned, for crop-spraying flights, and the central area re-opened to other light aircraft [1986]. The dummy deck survives, being preserved as a unique piece of aviation history, by owner Keith R.V. Pierson of Kedgeworth Limited, whose earthmoving machinery is now based at Henstridge Airfield in a landscape of wildlife lakes that are of his own creation.

HF — squadron code of 183 (Gold Coast) Squadron, flying rocket-firing Typhoons on cross-Channel missions from RAF Hurn [1-14 July 1944].

Hight — New Zealand **Pilot Officer Cecil Hight** [1917-1940] in a Spitfire of 234 Squadron from RAF Middle Wallop, was shot down and killed over Leven Avenue and Walsford Road, Bournemouth, in a Battle of Britain dog-fight [15 August 1940].

He is buried in Boscombe Cemetery, has a memorial plaque in St Peter's Church, and the post-war Pilot Hight Road was named in his honour.

Hinks — Spitfire flyer **Flying Officer C.O. Hinks** of RAF Warmwell was killed during the Battle of Britain [14 September 1940]. He is buried in the RAF plot at Warmwell churchyard.

HH — code letters of 175 Squadron, flying Hurricanes from RAF Warmwell [1942].

Hlavac — Czechoslovakian flyer **Sergeant Pilot Jaroslav Hlavac** [1914-1940] of 56 Squadron from RAF Boscombe Down was killed when a flight of Messerschmitt Bf.109 fighters shot down his Hurricane at Manor Farm, Worgret, west of Wareham [10 October 1940]. He had only been with the squadron for two days and is buried in the RAF plot at Warmwell churchyard.

Hogg — Spitfire flyer **Pilot Officer Edward Sydney Hogg** [died 1986] of 152 Squadron from Warmwell claimed a half share in the destruction of a Junkers Ju.88 bomber [23 August 1940]. He left the squadron two months later but remained in the Royal Air Force, leaving as Wing Commander at the end of the Second World War.

Hogg — Jersey-born Spitfire flyer **Pilot Officer Richard Malzard Hogg** [1919-40] of 152 Squadron from RAF Warmwell shared in the kills of two Junkers Ju.88 bombers [12 and 21 August 1940].

He was declared "Missing in Action" after being lost over the sea during a day of fierce Battle of Britain dog-fights [25 August 1940]. His body was not recovered.

Holland — Australian Spitfire flyer **Sergeant Pilot Kenneth Holland** from RAF Warmwell claimed a third share of 152 Squadron's kill of a Heinkel He.111 bomber off Portland [15 September 1940]. It probably belonged to Kampfgruppe 55 from Chartres.

He claimed a third share in the kill of a Junkers Ju.88 that was shot down at Ladywell Barn, Imber, Wiltshire, but sustained damage to hydraulic, glycol, and oil pipes [17 September 1940]. He crash-landed on the obstructed concrete runways of a disused aerodrome at Yatesbury.

Two days later he was vectored from Warmwell Aerodrome towards a Junkers Ju.88 bomber [19 September 1940]. Holland was Green One for the afternoon and his partner, Green Two, was left behind and below the cloud. Holland found the target above the cloud at 11,500 feet and fired a total of 2,800 rounds sending it into a vertical dive towards the sea, off the Isle of Wight, with both engines burning.

His next kill would prove doubly fatal. He brought down one of the

Heinkel He.111 bombers (G1+EP) of Kampfgruppe 55 that had devastated the Bristol Aeroplane Company's works at Filton. In doing so he was hit in the head by return fire and both aeroplanes crashed at Church Farm, Woolverton, Somerset [25 September 1940].

His body was cremated at Weymouth Crematorium.

Holmes — Spitfire flyer **Pilot Officer Frederick Henry Holmes** [1919-44] of 152 Squadron from RAF Warmwell claimed the destruction of Junkers Ju.87 [18 August 1940] and a share in the kill of a Junkers Ju.88 [21 August 1940]. Later in the war, as a Flight-Lieutenant with 487 Squadron, he was killed over Germany [4 December 1944] and is buried in the Reichswald War cemetery, near Cleves.

Horner — "Battle of the Beams" **Wing Commander G.K. Horner** of the Special Duties Flight from Christchurch Aerodrome searched out German blind-bombing navigation signals for the Telecommunications Research Establishment at Worth Matravers [1940-42]. He received the hand-over of the new Hurn Aerodrome from the contractors, on behalf of the Air Ministry and the Royal Air Force.

Horsa — troop-carrying glider, made by Airspeed Limited at its factory in Somerford, Christchurch. First used by airborne forces in the invasion of Sicily [9 July 1943], and then in mainland Europe, in Normandy on D-Day, at Arnhem, and landings inside Germany.

Howard — actor and film-maker **Leslie Howard** stayed at the King's Arms Hotel, Christchurch, whilst working on *The First of the Few*, dramatising the legend of the Spitfire [October 1941]. The film also starred Major David Niven and Rosamund John.

A grass airfield fitted the story of the fighter's creation, with Flight-Lieutenant Joseph "Mutt" Summers making the first flight of Reginald Joseph Mitchell's prototype K5054 from Eastleigh Aerodrome, Southampton [5 March 1936]. RAF Warmwell had been selected for the filming but Howard decided instead to utilise the new concrete runways at RAF Ibsley, near Ringwood, as being not only modern looking but technically easier for filming than having to contend with the eight-gun fighters bouncing up and down across the grass.

Howard-Williams — Spitfire flyer in *The First of the Few* **Wing Commander Peter Howard-Williams** [1921-93] retired to Redcotts Lane, Wimborne. During the filming, starring Leslie Howard and David Niven, he was stationed at RAF Ibsley [1941]. Reality was also action-packed at the time, with several kills of enemy aircraft over the New Forest and Dorset coast. He was awarded the Distinguished Flying Cross.

Howell — Spitfire flyer **Flight-Lieutenant Frank Jonathan Howell** [killed 1948] of 609 Squadron from RAF Warmwell parachuted into the sea after a dog-fight off Swanage [8 July 1940]. He would return to the sky for a succession of kills: Junkers Ju.87 [13 August 1940]; Junkers Ju.88 [15 August 1940]; Messerschmitt Bf.110 [7 September 1940]; Junkers Ju.87 [13 September 1940]; Dornier Do.17 [15 September 1940]; Messerschmitt Bf.110 [7 October 1940]; half a share of a Junkers Ju.88 [21 October 1940; 609 Squadron's hundredth victory].

Awarded the Distinguished Flying Cross [25 October 1940]. Posted to RAF Filton to form 118 Squadron [20 February 1941] and later to the Far East where he was captured by the Japanese after the sinking of the battleship HMS *Prince of Wales* [10 December 1941].

Post-war, Squadron Leader Howell would be decapitated by the wing of a Vampire as he was filming his jets [9 May 1948].

H2S — airborne "Town Finder" radar for blind bombing of German cities, devised by Group 8 of the Telecommunications Research Establishment, working from a Nissen hut in the grounds of the Establishment's eastern out-station, Leeson House at Langton Matravers [1941-42]. Given its name after Winston Churchill's chief scientific adviser, Professor Frederick Lindemann, snapped "It stinks!" upon hearing some excuses.

Tested above the Bournemouth conurbation by aircraft of the Telecommunications Flying Unit, initially from a Blenheim bomber flying from Christchurch Aerodrome and then on a specially adapted four-engined Halifax from RAF Hurn [17 April 1942].

Put into production in a top-secret factory beside Northbourne Golf Links at West Howe, Bournemouth. First used operationally, by Pathfinders, to drop flares on Hamburg for a major raid [30-31 January 1943]. Enabled night-bombing of the correct cities — previously Bomber Command had "attacked Hambourn in mistake for Essen" — for the duration of the Second World War.

Hughes-Rees — Spitfire flyer **Sergeant Pilot Anthony Hughes-Rees** [1920-43] of 609 Squadron from RAF Warmwell claimed the destruction of a Messerschmitt Bf.110 and then crash-landed his fighter, L1008 after suffering engine failure near Glastonbury [25 September 1940]. He had only been with the squadron a matter of days and would be awarded the Distinguished Flying Medal after increasing his tally to four kills [8 August 1941].

Hughes-Rees was killed in the Middle East, as a Flying Officer with 73 Operational Training Unit [30 April 1943], and is buried in Moascar War Cemetery, Egypt.

Hurn Aerodrome — built on a gravel plain north of the River Stour at Bournemouth, by the Air Ministry on behalf of the Royal Air Force, for 11 Group Fighter Command. Elevation 34 feet above sea level. Three concrete runways were constructed by various engineering firms and attracted their first Luftwaffe bombs at the close of the Battle of Britain [3 December 1940].

Before the war the site had been recommended to Bournemouth Corporation for a municipal aerodrome, by international aviator Sir Alan Cobham.

Three hardened concrete runways, initially 5,200 feet, 4,800 feet and 3,400 feet. Seven large and ten small blister hangars. Pundit Code "KU".

Handed from the contractors to the Air Ministry which passed it to 11 Group Fighter Command. The hand-over ceremony was to Wing Commander G.K. Horner of the Special Duties Flight, from Christchurch Aerodrome [1 August 1941].

Overseas Aircraft Despatch Units and Communications Flights operated from RAF Hurn [1942-44]. The first Liberator landed on 18 January

1942 and many more followed, to be flown onward via Gibraltar and across the Sahara Desert, to operational bases in the Middle East. This aircraft was the RAF version of the bulky high-wing Consolidated B-24 bomber which was powered by four Pratt and Whitney 1,200 horsepower Twin Wasp engines. It became the largest single United States aircraft type of World War Two, 18,482 being delivered, of which the RAF received 1,889.

Hurn became the base—with a large hardened hangar that still survives—for Prime Minister Winston Churchill's personal Liberator and other VIP aircraft [July 1942].

RAF Hum had then been transferred from Fighter Command to 38 Wing Army Co-operation Command, with its commanding officer being Group Captain Harold John Granville Ellis Proud [1 June 1942]. The station provided transport support for the 1st Airborne Division.

A flight of six VIP Flying Fortresses, one of which was left behind with failed undercarriage hydraulics, took off from RAF Hurn [3 November 1942] with Lieutenant-General Dwight D. Eisenhower and the staff officers of Allied Forces North-West Africa, taking them to the conference in Gibraltar that approved the detailed plans for the invasion of French North Africa.

A total of 180 transport aircraft, including 51 C47 Dakota troop car-riers and 61 Boeing B-17F Flying Fortress bombers, passed through Hurn in Operation Cackle, which was the Hurn-Gibraltar air ferry service that was completed without a single casualty. It provided large elements of the logistical back-up for Operation Torch, in which a combined British and American force involving a total of 107,000 men landed in French North Africa at Casablanca, Oran, and Algiers [8 November 1942].

Throughout 1942 work was carried out on the ground, and tested in the air around Hurn, on modifications to bombers such as the Halifax, Whitley, and Stirling, into tow-craft for gliders carrying airborne troops and equipment. In 1943 the Whitleys were replaced by twin-engined Albemarles, the first British military aircraft with a tricycle under-cariage. The unit would remain at Hurn until D-Day.

The aerodrome's main user, No.38 Wing, Army Co-Operation Command, was reformed as No.38 Group, Airborne Forces [11 October 1943].

Control of Hurn and its 38 Group operators was passed to the Allied Expeditionary Air Force [1 February 1944] in preparation for the invasion of Europe. Massive expansion in capacity was already underway with the two main runways at Hurn being increased in length by half as much again and a square mile of heathland on the north and east sides was churned into a moonscape of yellow sand, crossed by the curves and frying-pan shapes of a complex network of dispersal areas.

Swarms of escort fighters took off or landed back at RAF Hurn throughout the months preceding the invasion of Normandy. This activity was in full swing by the end of the previous year, with 24 Spitfires escorting bombers to Triqueville [22 December 1943] and 37 P-47 Thunderbolts of the United States Army Air Force protecting Liberator bombers taking part in attacks on the Cherbourg peninsula [29 December 1943]. Two flak-damaged B-17 Flying Fortresses also came into Hurn. The station participated in actions that succeeded during the month in destroying eight V1 flying bomb launch sites.

83 Group at Hurn was augmented with an additional three Typhoon squadrons, forming 124 Wing [April 1944].

Crucially, 28 Hurn Typhoons would deliver 96 60-lb rockets and seven tons of bombs on German coastal radar stations; with the deliberate exception of that at Fécamp which was kept intact so that it could report spoof activity aimed at convincing the enemy that the main thrust of the invasion would come further up-Channel, east of the Seine [5 June 1944].

P-61 Black Widow night-fighters of the 9th United States Army Air Force and B-26 Marauders of the American 97th Bombardment Group also operated from Hurn Aerodrome during the D-Day campaign.

After the Mosquitoes quit Hurn, to be redeployed at Middle Wallop [1 August 1944], they were replaced by Martin B-26 Marauders of 596, 597, and 598 Squadrons of the 9th Bombardment Group of the United States Army Air Force [23 August 1944]. Their achievements included a spectacular raid on the railway marshalling yards at Corbiel to the south of Paris [14 August 1944]. They were soon to be moved across the Channel to a forward base in Normandy [20 August 1944].

With the transfer of British Overseas Airways Corporation's landplane operations from Lyneham, Wiltshire, Hurn had the distinction of being Britain's principal civilian airfield.

Civilian operations at what was still RAF Hurn began with the arrival of G-AGJI, a Lancaster transporter of British Overseas Airways Corporation which flew in from Lyneham, Wiltshire [20 January 1944]. More followed, as did the post-war Lancastrians, and Hurn became BOAC's main British base for solid-runway airliners.

BOAC Avro York MW103, given the civilian letters G-AGJA, flew the first wartime service from Hurn to Cairo, via Morocco and across the Sahara Desert [22 April 1944].

The first Lancastrian of BOAC's new fleet, G-AGLF, carried the markings of the RAF's South-East Asia theatre for its 53-hour proving flight from Hurn to Sydney, Australia [23 - 26 April 1945].

History would be made with the arrival from La Guardia Airport, New York, of a military C-54 Skymaster of Pan American Airways, at the end of a 17-hour flight [18 September 1945]. This was the first time a four-engined land-plane — as distinct from a flying-boat — crossed the Atlantic Ocean on civilian service.

Post-war international flights from Hurn began with BOAC Lancastrian G-AGLV inaugurating the 12,000-miles service to Sydney, Australia [30 May 1945]. Pan American Airways arrived from the opposite direction, with an ex-military C54 Skymaster in a 17-hour flight from New York. British Halifax bombers, converted into Haltons, took over the old flying-boat run, to Nigeria. Then BOAC Lancastrian G-AGMG made its maiden long-haul flight, from Hurn to Buenos Aires [9-18 October 1945]. Avro York G-AGNT took the first 7,000-miles run out of Hurn to Malta and the Middle East and then virtually from Cairo to the Cape, with intermediate stops at Khartoum and Nairobi and destination Johannesburg in South Africa [10 November 1945].

South African Airways shared that route and the Atlantic run was also serviced by American Export Lines and American Overseas Airways. Free Europe entered the running with Koninkijke Luchtvaart Maatschappij, from The Netherlands, and Sabena.

The Americans consolidated their hold of the big airframes of the Atlantic run with the "service of the future" as it was hailed when Lockheed Constellation made its first ocean crossing and deposited 29 passengers from New York on the tarmac at Hurn after a flight of only 12 hours [1 January 1946]. All that

Britain had to offer in competition were the Clipper flying-boats, also American airframe, on the run from Poole Harbour to Baltimore, but these could no longer compete against the landplanes and the service was abandoned [7 March 1946].

Pan American was winning world prizes with the Constellation which was set to achieve the first commercial flight "Round-the-Globe" [29 June 1947]. Its landplanes were also targeting the chunks of Empire that were not British; such as the Belgian Congo.

All that BOAC and Hurn had to compete with were the N-class Lancastrians, but at least these were coming through in quantity. Some 21 would be delivered [1946-48] and they ousted Dakotas from the mid-range hauls to Africa and India. Fourteen were named, for "N" names from *Nelson* and *Nairn* to *Natal* and *Nepal*.

A further 14 Lancastrians were seconded to British South American Airways, an operating company owned by BOAC, and given their own series of *Star* names. Rather than being celestial names these had the key word first and ranged from *Star Dust* to *Star Watch*. The former would crash in the Andes and the latter was wrecked on a training flight into what was still being called Heath Row. Overall it was a successful subsidiary, with its own charismatic chairman, Air Vice-Marshal Donald "Pathfinder" Bennett [1945-48] who led from the top and flew geographical survey flights across the sub-continent.

Hurn's international rôle was now threatened as operators were given a new horizon, on the meadows of Heath Row in Middlesex which had been elevated to the status of London Airport [February 1948].

Hurn was no longer centre-stage but it remained in the forefront of technology. Flight Refuelling Limited acquired a fleet of Lancastrians as they were withdrawn from passenger flights. The School of Air Traffic Control turned aerial traffic management into an art, teaching radar, blind-landing, and queue stacking techniques [1949-62]. The planemakers also arrived, with Vickers Armstrong (Aircraft) Limited flight-testing the first V-bomber, the Vickers Valiant, and setting up a factory to produce their passenger project, which became the Vickers Viscount with work shared between Weybridge and Hurn. Two hundred were built at Hurn.

What was now called Bournemouth (Hurn) Airport also gave a home to Airwork Services who were civilian providers of target-towing flights for the Fleet Air Arm [1952]. Theirs was a general collection of

DORSET AVIATION ENCYCLOPÆDIA

aircraft-carrier machines plus the versatile Mosquito.

Surprise passenger arrivals became increasingly frequent as the notorious smogs closed London Airport and weather conditions often prevented Blackbushe from being used as an alternative. Hurn was second in line for diverted flights.

Commonest aircraft at Hurn and over Bournemouth at the end of the 1950s was the Bristol 170 Wayfarer, otherwise known as the Bristol Freighter. This owed its bulbous lines to the Hamilcar gliders that had carried airborne forces from Hurn and Tarrant Rushton during the Second World War. All that seemed different was that it had a pair of engines and the camouflage had given way to the sleek liveries of Silver City Airways and Jersey Airlines; this was the first aerial car-ferry.

Transfers of operations from Eastleigh brought British European Airways and British United Airways, as well as Air Safari and Cambrian Airways to Hurn, with a consequent surge in the number of passengers. High summer in 1961 saw the 50,000 barrier broken for the first time and there was another monthly first for Hurn — that of 1,000 airbone cars [August 1961].

Passengers accommodation was grossly inadequate by modern standards and these expectations were met by the building of a new terminal near the south-east corner of the airfield, at a cost of £250,000 [1963].

Vickers had become a division of the British Aircraft Corporation and their first BAC 1-11, made at Hurn, lifted off to begin a new age of civilian aviation [20 August 1963]. By the time the last of its final version was completed, in the 1-11 475-series, the factory was part of British Aerospace plc [May 1984]. The following month, on news that maintenance work was insufficient to keep it open, the Hurn works was closed.

British European Airways continued to use Hurn until their last scheduled flights in a Vickers Viscount to Jersey [31 March 1966]. The cream of the business was now in package tours and these were seen as the new mass-market opportunity. Channel Airways filled the missing link with Dorset's offshore islands — which traditionally regarded Weymouth as their principal mainland port. They also maintained the French connection with a triangle of services that extended to Paris.

Express Air Services and British Island Airways also crossed the Channel and a network of internal flights to British cities was provided by

Dan Air, with a fleet of Hawker-Siddeley 748s. Hurn also turned out qualified pilots, through the College of Air Training. The Air Traffic Control Evaluation Unit experimented with advanced prototypes of new radars, using the Hurn flights as guinea pigs — though separately from the airfield's actual air traffic system.

The Fleet Requirements Unit moved from Hurn to the Royal Naval Air Station at Yeovilton [1972]. Channel Express became a new name on the Channel Islands run, with Dart Heralds.

Flight Refuelling Limited, having moved its fleet of tankers from Tarrant Rushton to Hurn, expanded into the executive jet business, with a squadron of sleek fighter-like Dassault Falcons, augmented by Cessna Conquests [1988].

That, for now, is the history and the present lies with Bournemouth International Airport as Hurn (Bournemouth) Airport — the 1941-built Hurn Aerodrome — was renamed at the end of the decade [1989].

Hurn crashes — flak-damaged Whirlwind P6983 of 263 Squadron from RAF Filton, Gloucestershire, force-landed at the new RAF Hurn with one engine out of action and the other leaking glycol coolant, after having claimed two Messerschmitt Bf.109s off Cherbourg [6 August 1941].

Spitfire EB687 was written-off on arrival at Hurn, for escort duty, when it collided with a parked Whitley bomber [10 July 1943].

The crew of a Whitley tug-plane were killed when it stalled on take-off and crashed inside the perimeter fence, in what should have been a routine training flight from RAF Hurn [July 1943].

One Sunday afternoon four gliders, of the type used for carrying airborne troops, crashed into the lane leading to East Parley mission church, immediately west of the Hurn Aerodrome [1943].

Hurricane LD972 of 439 (Royal Canadian Air Force) Squadron crashed two miles east of RAF Hurn, into the Avon valley, after colliding with an American P-47 Thunderbolt from USAAF Christchurch that had thrown itself into Canadian practice dog-fights [21 March 1944]. Flight-Lieutenant Norval E. Pollock was killed.

The prototype Airspeed Ambassador, newly made at the firm's Christchurch works, landed with the undercarriage retracted, at Hurn, during a practice emergency which became real [January 1950]. One engine had been shut off during take-off to see how she handled. The pilot was George Errington.

Clever aerobatics, a touch too ambitious, caused the spectacular crash of an Argentinian Pampa 1A-63 advanced jet trainer that was practising at Hurn for the Farnborough Air Show [31 August 1992]. Falklands veterans Commander Juan Carlos Sapolsky and Captain Omar Darion Gelardi were killed instantly as the aircraft "dropped like a stone" and hit the ground with "an incredible bang", followed by a fireball.

Witness Gordon Ansty said that something had gone wrong with what was obviously intended as their party piece for the air display: "Their plane kept trying one particularly dangerous trick where it flew up to about 1,000-feet and then dive-bombed vertically, before pulling up at the last minute."

Mrs Lucy Lucas of Merritown Farm said the blue and silver-coloured trainer had been going into spiral dives: "It did two and then it did a third one and the engine seemed to cut out."

Hurricane L1592 — one of three stationed at Christchurch Aerodrome to protect the Special Duties Flight which operated there [194042]. This particular machine survived the war and became part of the National Aeronautical Collection that is displayed by the Science Museum in London.

Hythe class — ex-military flying-boats of British Overseas Airways Corporation, gathered in Poole Harbour and named for the resumption of civilian services to Singapore and Australia [January 1946].

Comprised *Hadfield, Hailsham, Halstead, Hamble, Hamilton, Hanwell, Harlequin, Harwich, Haslemere, Hawkesbury, Henley, Himalaya, Hobart, Honduras, Hotspur, Howard, Hudson, Hungerford, Hunter, Huntingdon,* and *Hythe* (being named for BOAC's past and future home-base on Southampton Water).

Apart from Hailsham, which crashed in Poole Harbour 14 March 1946], and some overseas losses, the survivors returned to Hythe [31 March 1948]. A succession of sales and scrappings led to the total withdrawal of British flying-boat services [30 September 1958].

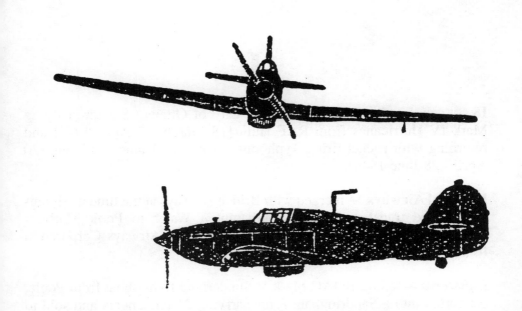

Hurricane: the other famous fighter of the Battle
of Britain crashed all over Dorset in the summer
of 1940 as squadrons from Hampshire, Wiltshire
and above all RAF Exeter, came
to the aid of hard-pressed
Spitfires from RAF Warmwell

I

I8 — squadron code of 440 (RCAF City of Ottawa) Squadron flying Mark IV Hurricanes from RAF Hum [18 March - 3 April 1944] and returning with rocket-firing Typhoons for cross-Channel missions [20 April - 28 June 1944].

Imperial Airways — merged with British Airways at the time its flying-boats were transferred from Southampton Water to Poole Harbour [August 1939], and operated as British Overseas Airways Corporation from the new year [1 January 1940].

Inglaterra — an ex-BOAC Mark V Sunderland flying-boat from Poole, converted into a Sandringham-3 for carrying 21 passengers and sold to the Argentine airline Dodero [November 1945].

Inness — Spitfire pilot **Flying Officer Richard Frederick Inness** of 152 Squadron from RAF Warmwell, who had left Eton to join the RAF [August 1938], claimed the destruction of a Junkers Ju.88 [26 September 1940], and then a Messerschmitt Bf.109 [27 September 1940].

He became an instructor with 53 Operational Training Unit at RAF Heston [spring 1941] and then commanded 130 Squadron [October 1943], followed by 222 Squadron [February 1944]. Left the RAF as a Squadron Leader [1946].

Isle of Purbeck Light Aeroplane Club — founded by Lieutenant Colonel Louis Strange DSO, MC, DFC and operating from Swanage Aerodrome [1926] which was located in Strange's home parish, between Worth Matravers and St Alban's Head. Flying Officer H.W.R. Banting was the club's chief instructor.

Air Vice-Marshal Sir Sefton Brancker [1877-1930], the Director of Civil Aviation at the Air Ministry, visited the club [23 August 1926]. He was picked up from Hendon in the club's Simmonds Spartan biplane and taken on to Dorchester for the formation meeting of Dorsetshire Aero Club.

Iwerne Minster crash — at The Beeches, beside the main road, of a Messerschmitt Bf.110 (S9+DU) after engine damage in a dog-fight [27 September 1940]. Belonging to Erprobungsgruppe 210, an experimental proving unit from Cherbourg, it had been attempting to take part in an abortive raid on the Parnall Aircraft Company at Yate, near Chipping Sodbury. Pilot Friedrich Ebner made a successful crash-landing but the gunner, Werner Zwick, was taken to Shaftesbury Hospital with major wounds.

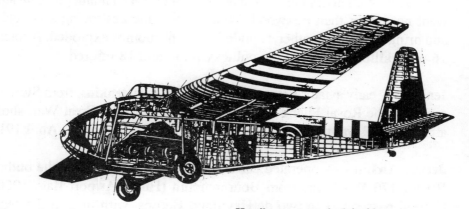

Hamilcar: cutaway look inside
the wooden glider that was the
heavyweight carrier of airborne forces
from RAF Tarrant Rushton

Halifax: four-engined tug-plane for the Hamilcar
glider, which lead the aerial armada that took off
from Tarrant Rushton to begin the D-Day landings
in Normandy

J

James — hapless pilot **Lieutenant Vincent R. James** [1920-40] of 509th Squadron of the 405th Fighter Bomber Group of the United States Army Air Force failed in his take-off from Christchurch Aerodrome and crashed in Foxwood Avenue, Mudeford [06.45 hours, 29 June 1944].

Then at 14.00 hours the same day, in another P-47 Thunderbolt, he again went no further than Foxwood Avenue, this time destroying a bungalow and bringing down another Thunderbolt as his bombs exploded. A total of 16 were killed, including the unlucky pilot, and 18 injured.

Jenkins — early aviator **Lieutenant-Colonel Leslie Jenkins**, from Swanage, served in the Royal Flying Corps and was killed in the Great War, shortly after the RFC was re-titled and became the Royal Air Force [1 April 1918].

Jersey Airlines — operated car-carrying Bristol Freighters, the bulbous Bristol 170 Wayfarer, from Bournemouth (Hurn) Airport [late 1950s]. Carried passengers in two de Havilland Herons, with one on the Jersey service and the other going to Guernsey.

Jet Heritage Limited — refurbished historic aircraft, overhauling the avioics and repainting in authentic colours, in workshops at Bournemouth International Airport. Some of their commissions have local associations, such as Christchurch-made de Havilland Vampires T.55 G-BVLM and FB.6 G-BVPO that were given the camouflage of 2 Squadron, Royal Jordan Air Force, before being handed over to the newly formed Royal Jordanian Historic Flight [1995].

The FB.6 was a former target-tug in the Swiss Air Force. Its overhaul was carried out by Eric Hayward and his team. Its place in the workshops was taken by Hawker Hunter F.6A XG160 which had been handed over to the Jordanians at RAF Scampton.

Their classic restoration — Hurn-based and a frequent visitor to air shows — is Armstrong Whitworth Meteor NF.11, G-LOSM/ WM167 which was delivered to the RAF [1952], though it never went into squadron service. Its extended nose, being 47 inches longer than the F.8 fighter, housed an Airborne Interception (AI) Mark 10 radar. This was fitted as standard in the NF.11 which became the RAF's first jet-powered night-fighter.

Johnson — aviatrix **Amy Johnson** [1903-1941] landed to a hero's welcome at Talbot Farm, Bournemouth [27 August 1930]. It was four months after she had become the first woman to fly solo from London to Australia, breaking en route the record for a flight between London and India, by touching down in Karachi in six days. Her arrival in Bournemouth, where she transferred to Sir William Morris's best car, was for the purpose of opening a fête in Meyrick Park.

Jones — Spitfire flyer **Pilot Officer John Sinclair Bucknall Jones** [1918-1940] of 152 Squadron from RAF Warmwell was shot down by Messerschmitt Bf.109s in the middle of the English Channel [11 August 1940]. He baled out of R6614 but drowned, being buried in Sainte Marie Cemetery, Le Havre.

Joubert — controller of the RAF's wartime radar and signals intelligence operations **Air Marshal Sir Philip Joubert** [died 1965] lived at Canford Cliffs. Nominally the commanding officer of Combined Operations at Poole this was a cover for his main task. In effect he controlled the Telecommunications Research Establishment at Worth Matravers, through the scientific Battle of the Beams. The Luftwaffe unknowingly had its revenge with a bomb that fell on his house, though he was out at the time [March 1941].

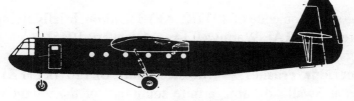

Horsa: glider for airborne forces, made by Airspeed
at Christchurch and based at RAF Hurn and
Tarrant Rushton, going to war in Normandy
and at Arnhem

K

Kay — airborne chaplain **Rev. George Alexander Kay** was killed on D-Day while tending the wounded in Normandy [6 June 1944]. "His father served the church and parish during the war years," a plaque records in Shapwick parish church.

Kearsey — Spitfire flyer **Sergeant Pilot Albert Wallace "Bill" Kearsey** of 152 Squadron from RAF Warmwell claimed a Messerschmitt Bf.110 kill [30 September 1940]. He shared with Pilot Officer Eric "Boy" Marrs the destruction of a Junkers Ju.88 bomber which they found over the Blackmore Vale and put down on a cobbler's shed at Poole [14 November 1940]. Kearsey survived the war.

Kennedy — Australian volunteer **Flight Lieutenant John Connelly Kennedy** [1917-40], flying a Hurricane of 238 Squadron from Middle Wallop, Hampshire, crashed to his death at Little Mayne Farm, West Knighton, after a dog-fight [13 July 1940]. He is buried in the RAF plot at RAF Warmwell.

Keymer — Bournemouth car salesman **Sergeant Pilot Michael Keymer** [1916-40], the son of Eastleigh's vicar, joined 65 Squadron at RAF Hornchurch [7 August 1940]. He shared in the destruction of a Messerschmitt Bf.109 a week later but was then shot down, in Spitfire K9909, over the Straits of Dover [22 August 1940]. He is buried on the other side of the Channel, in the churchyard at Bazinghen, France.

KH — squadron code of 403 (RCAF) Squadron, briefly flying Mark XVI Spitfires from RAF Warmwell [4 - 14 January 1945].

Kimmeridge crashes — Messerschmitt Bf.110 (L1+FZ) crashed in flames at Swalland Farm, a mile south-east of the village on the Luftwaffe's routed Adlertag (Eagle Day) attack [13 August 1940]. It belonged to Lehrgeschwader 1, a unit formed to test new aircraft of all types, and innovative tactics, under operational conditions.

Another Bf.110 (3U+DS), belonging to Zerostörergeschwader 26, the Geschwader named Horst Wessel after the Nazi writer of a militant anti-Semitic song which became a national anthem, crash-landed near Gaulter Gap [27 September 1940]. It had three "kill" bars, denoting victories over RAF aircraft. Crewmen Fritz Schupp and Karl Nechwatal were taken prisoner. Their Bf.110, which had been taking part in an abortive raid on the Parnall Aircraft Company at Yate, near Chipping Sodbury, was claimed by Spitfires from RAF Warmwell.

Kingston Russell crash — into Brickhills Field, near Kingston Russell House, of a Messerschmitt Bf.110C (3U+JP) belonging to the 6th Staffel of Zerstörergeschwader 26 [16.00 hours, 7 October 1940]. It had been defending the bombers en route to the Westland Aircraft Company works at Yeovil. Crewmen Obergefreiter Herbert Schilling and Oberfeldwebel Karl Herzog were killed on impact.

Further human remains were removed, together with wreckage and identification papers, during an excavation carried out by Andy Saunders [1976]. The flyers' grave is in the German war cemetery at Cannock Chase.

Kirkpatrick — early aviator **Lieutenant Yvone Kirkpatrick** [1899-1975] of Oaklands, Rowlands Hill, Wimborne, joined the Royal Flying Corps [May 1917]. He graduated to a Sopwith Camel on being posted to the Western Front, to join 203 Squadron at Izel le Hameau, near Arras [May 1918]. He had numerous close encounters and at least one crash landing but his worst couple of hours were in the last Allied air offensive [noon, 26 September 1918] when the squadron lost five aircraft on an attack on an aerodrome eleven miles inside German lines. He dropped his bombs, used all his ammunition, and then ran into problems. "Archie", incidentally, means anti-aircraft fire: "I decided to come home. The Archie was awful, along with machine-gun fire on the ground. I was trying to climb up to some of our machines which were going west, when suddenly there was a bang and my engine stopped."

It restarted from his gravity petrol tank, but he was still in trouble. "My engine wasn't going very well and the wind was against me. You should have seen the expression on people's faces. I went over a sunken road and saw two fat old Huns walking calmly along with their hands in their pockets; they simply stared at me with their mouths open. Then I saw two Fokkers up above diving at me. I simply tore round trees and churches with them firing at me."

On landing after the machine gun fire had stopped, among Scottish troops, he found he "had a bullet through my tank, the petrol was pouring out". Things continued to be "rather too exciting now" as the British divisions pushed on through the Hindenburg Line during the following week.

Post-war he took up teaching and spent 33 years at Canford School, between Wimborne and Poole.

Klein—Polish Spitfire flyer **Sergeant Pilot Zygmunt Klein** [1918-40] of 152 Squadron from RAF Warmwell damaged a Messerschmitt Bf.110 in a dog-fight [7 October 1940]. He ran out of petrol and successfully force-landed on the Devon coast [26 November 1940]. Then "just disappeared" in P9427 over Poole Bay, during a fierce series of engagements with Messerschmitt Bf.109 fighters [28 November 1940]. His body was not recovered.

KS — code letters of the Station Flight at RAF Tarrant Rushton.

KU — pundit code for RAF Hurn, on ten feet high white letters at the airfield and flashed at night in red light Morse code, from a Pundit mobile beacon some miles from the station.

Lightning:
P-38 fighter-bomber
of the USAAF, based
at RAF Warmwell,
found 'targets of opportunity'
across northern France

L

Langar — Luftwaffe ace **Hauptmann Langar**, the officer commanding the elite pathfinder Kampfgruppe 100, was killed when his Heinkel He.111 plunged into a hillside near Shaftesbury in low cloud [23 May 1942]. He was trying to evade Squadron Leader John "Cat's Eyes" Cunningham, in a Beaufighter of 604 Squadron from RAF Middle Wallop, in an interception directed by Sopley radar station.

Langton Herring crashes — of Westland Wallace K6063, belonging to 6 Air Training Corps, whilst dropping a drogue over the Chesil Beach Bombing Range [10 March 1939].

A similar drogue-dropping mishap caused the loss of Fairey Seal K3480 from 10 Bombing and Gunnery School at RAF Warmwell [22 April 1940].

Other losses on the range, not identified with a specific parish, are listed under the entry for Chesil Beach crashes.

Langton Matravers crashes — Spitfire R6811 of 152 Squadron from RAF Warmwell successfully crash-landed at Spyway Farm after a Battle of Britain dog-fight [8 August 1940]. It was flown by Pilot Officer Walter Beaumont.

There was drama of a different kind when what should have been an epic endurance flight from Creech Barrow Hill ended with *Balloon Gerard Heineken* bringing down power cables at Coles Farm, Langton Matravers [25 July 1975].

Lindbergh Road — street close to Castle Lane in the suburb of Moordown, Bournemouth, named for pioneer aviator Colonel Charles Augustus Lindbergh whose *Spirit of St Louis* made the first non-stop crossing of the Atlantic [20-21 May 1927]. Renamed Franklin Road by Bournemouth town councillors, after Lindbergh expressed pro-Nazi sentiments [January 1943]. Its new name was that of the Anglophile wartime American president, Franklin Delano Roosevelt.

Lindsay Hall — in Lindsay Road, Bournemouth, was the home of the seventh Baron Ventry [1898-1987], Britain's leading post-war expert on airships.

Demolished and rebuilt as quality flats [1992], called Ventry Court.

Littlebredy Relief Landing Ground — established courtesy Lady Williams of Bridehead [1972] on the high chalk plateau south of the village (Ordnance Survey map reference SY 682 743). Receiving up to four Portland helicopters at a time it specialised in handling and hovering.

Loders crash — of a new Zero Airship, on an anti-submarine patrol from Mullion, Cornwall, which was heading inland towards the Admiralty Airship Station at Powerstock [summer 1917]. It came too low after passing over Bridport and clipped treetops, coming down on a grassy slope above the branch railway line. Bombs were safely jettisoned and the pilot, John Owner, and his crew suffered only minor bruising.

Lovell-Gregg — heroic New Zealand Hurricane pilot **Squadron Leader Terence Lovell-Gregg** of 87 Squadron, from RAF Exeter, was killed at Abbotsbury during the height of the Battle of Britain [15 August 1940]. Roland Beamont, one of his pilots, returned with the story of how 27-year-old "Shovel" led his men into a mass of German aircraft at 18,000 feet over the sea off Portland. Ignoring adverse odds of fifteen-to-one, he told his men over the radio: "Come on chaps, let's surround them!"

He set about doing the impossible, leading the five of 87 Squadron's Hurricanes which were its only air-worthy machines: "Lovell-Gregg flew straight at the centre of the formation without hesitation or deviation in any way." Shot and burning, he attempted to glide to a crash-landing in The Fleet lagoon, but clipped an oak in the wood beside Abbotsbury Swannery and fell to his death. He is buried in the RAF plot at Warmwell churchyard.

LS — code letters of 297 (Army Co-Operation) Squadron, flying Whitleys from RAF Hurn [1942].

Lulworth crashes — Hurricane P3585 of 213 Squadron from RAF Exeter crash-landed on the "C" Range, Lulworth Camp, after engaging the Luftwaffe [11 August 1940]. Sergeant Pilot Ernest Snowden was unhurt and his fighter repairable.

Jubilant anti-aircraft gunners at Lulworth Camp brought down a Messerschmitt Bf.110 fighter-bomber during a major Battle of Britain attack [27 September 1940]. The stricken aircraft crashed to the ground about a thousand yards from the sea. It had been seen taking part in the abortive raid on the Parnall Aircraft Company at Yate, near Chipping Sodbury.

Another Bf.110, apparently belonging to Zerstörergeschwader 26 and involved in the attack on the Westland Aircraft factory at Yeovil, crashed into the sea 2,000 yards off Arish Mell Gap [7 October 1940]. It was claimed by Spitfires of 609 Squadron from RAF Warmwell.

Spitfire R6639 of 53 Operational Training Unit crashed at West Lulworth whilst attempting a forced-landing [10 September 1941].

There was a huge explosion as a Focke Wulf 190 came in low from over the sea, apparently misjudging its position, and flew straight into the side of Bindon Hill [21 October 1941].

Lutz — Luftwaffe veteran **Hauptmann Martin Lutz** [1913-40] led the abortive raid on the Parnall Aircraft Company at Yate, near Chipping Sodbury, crashed to his death at Bussey Stool Farm, near Tarrant Gunville [27 September 1940]. The Bf.110 fighter-bomber had been crippled over Bristol. He had served in the Condor Legion in the Spanish Civil War.

Lyme Bay Bombing Range — six miles off Lyme Regis, covering 16 square miles of sea, designated by the Air Ministry for daylight use [August 1939]. An initial limit of 120-lb was imposed on live bombs that could be dropped.

Lyme Bay crashes — numerous Battle of Britain losses from both sides, principally of the Luftwaffe but also defending Hurricanes from RAF Exeter and Spitfires of RAF Warmwell, fell into the sea off the Chesil Beach and Lyme Regis. For the remainder of the war an RAF Air-Sea Rescue launch operated from Lyme Regis. Some days they fell in twos, such as Hurricanes P3766 of 238 Squadron and P3082 of 501 Squadron shot down in the same dog-fight [20 July 1940].

An RAF Canberra bomber crashed into the sea at Lyme Bay during target-towing trials. Two of the crew were killed and one saved [1 May 1970].

Lytchett Matravers crash — Hawker Hind K5382 of the Royal Air Force College crashed near the village, during a low-flying flight that was foiled by pylon cables [26 April 1940].

Lytchett Minster crash — of an American B-17 Flying Fortress, returning from a cross-Channel mission, at Tatchell's Holding on Charity Farm, opposite the Baker's Arms [2 April 1942]. It was a successful emergency landing, followed by the arrival of heavy earth-moving machinery to make a temporary runway, which enabled the bomber to take off, after repairs and refuelling.

Lysander: produced by the local planemakers,
Westland Aircraft Limited at Yeovil, slipped across
the Channel on missions for the Special Operations
Executive, from RAF Tarrant Rushton

M

Machold — Luftwaffe ace **Oberleutnant Werner Machold**, Staffel-kapitän of the 7th Gruppe of Jagdeschwader 2 Richthofen, who had been credited with the fighter wing's hundredth victory over France and was personally congratulated by Field Marshal Hermann Göring, crash-landed at Worth Matravers [6 June 1941]. He was taken prisoner of war.

Maia **(G-ADHK)** — British Overseas Airways Corporation Short "Empire" flying-boat, converted to a C-class flying-boat [1940] and based at Poole. She had previously been a pioneering composite aircraft as the mother craft, with a cradle above her wings, for the Mercury mail-carrying floatplane. Destroyed in Poole Harbour by a Heinkel He.111 bomber G1+ES belonging to the 8th Staffel of the 3rd Gruppe, Kampfgeschwader 55, which would be brought down in the attack, off Arne, by anti-aircraft fire.

Malcolm — air-girl **Miss Betty Malcolm** [1913-36], of Glenmorag, Haig Avenue, Canford Cliffs, Poole, was burnt to death when her aeroplane crashed into a hangar at Alicante, Spain [January 1936]. She was pre-paring for an attempt on the solo record for the flight between England and Australia.

"I was afraid that Betty would kill herself, but she would not listen," her mother, Edith Malcolm, told the Daily Mail. "She pointed to the splendid flights she had made all over Europe since she learned to fly about three years ago, and said she was determined to become famous. Betty would rush off at a moment's notice without telling anybody where she was going and, with only a few things flung hastily into a suitcase, disappear in her plane across the Channel for weeks on end."

Her father was Brigadier-General Henry Huntly Leith Malcolm [1860-1938].

Manston crash — of Whitley bomber T4299 of 51 Squadron, from RAF

Dishforth, Yorkshire, outward bound to attack German battle-cruisers at Brest, brought down at Connegar Farm [3 April 1941]. Sergeant W.N. Brindley was killed but the other four members of the crew baled out successfully. The interception was found to be a case of friendly fire, resulting from misidentification of the twin-engined bomber, and traced to a Hurricane night-fighter, V6960, of 87 Squadron from RAF Exeter.

Mantle — fatally wounded pom-pom gunner **Jack Mantle** [1917-40] continued firing as "Stuka" dive-bombers sank anti-aircraft auxiliary HMS *Foylebank* in Portland Harbour. His legs had been shattered as bombs tore the ship apart. Of her 179 crew, 59 were killed and 60 injured in the attack, which came at the height of the Battle of Britain, on 4 July 1940. Leading Seaman Mantle from Southampton had gone to school at Affpuddle. He is buried in Portland Naval Cemetery, on the Verne Common hillside overlooking the dockyard and harbour and would be gazetted for the Victoria Cross — the first to be won for the Royal Navy inside territorial waters.

Marrs — youthful hero **Pilot Officer Eric Simcox "Boy" Marrs**, flying a Spitfire which he named "Old Faithful", with 152 Squadron from RAF Warmwell had his first "kill" disallowed [16 August 1940]. He had his machine covered with oil from it, in a dog-fight over the Isle of Wight, and insisted on claiming the Heinkel He.111: "I don't think it could have got home and I'm pretty sure it didn't. I am counting that as my first."

He put a Junkers Ju.87 "Stuka" of Stukageschwader 77 into the sea off Sussex two day's later, in a kill that was confirmed [18 August 1940]. Later that afternoon he went "Tally-ho" again in his second scramble of the day, this time off Portland, and thought he had accounted for a Dornier Do.17, but it managed to limp back to France.

Leading Blue Section, Marrs claimed a third share in the kill of a Junkers Ju.88 that was shot down at Ladywell Barn, Imber, Wiltshire, only three miles from his old school, Dauntsey's [17 September 1940]. Return fire from the stricken bomber smashed his Spitfire's air-cooler and forced him to crash-land at Yatesbury, on the concrete runways of a disused RAF training aerodrome.

Marrs was then parted from "Old Faithful" — in which he had flown 130 hours — though it would also survive to fly again, after restoration and now with a training unit.

Not that this would cramp his style. His next kill was his most flamboyant. Finding a lone Junkers Ju.88 at 23,000 feet above Somerset, he chased it across Exmoor and brought it down to within 50 feet of the hilltops, with ethylene glycol streaming from both engines [27 September 1940]. The stricken bomber reached the Bristol Channel and landed on the beach at Porlock: "I circled round and watched the crew get out. They waved to me and I waved back, and then hordes of civilians came rushing up. I watched the crew taken prisoner, beat up the beach, and then climbed away."

Three days later Marrs had to turn back to Warmwell Aerodrome for his own forced-landing, after German aircraft crippled his Spitfire [30 September 1940]: "I hopped out and went to the MO to get a lot of metal splinters picked out of my leg and wrist. I felt jolly glad to be down on the ground without having caught fire."

He would lead Blue Section at 20,000 feet over the eastern Frome valley on the day that the Luftwaffe did succeed in reaching the Westland Aircraft factory at Yeovil, killing a hundred civilian workers in a direct hit on an air-raid shelter [7 October 1940]. Marrs picked off the last Messerschmitt Bf.110 fighter-bomber of Zerstörergeschwader 26 in an exposed line. It went into the sea and the crew drifted down on to land: "Their parachutes streamed and opened and they began drifting slowly earthwards. Their aeroplane, left to itself, dived vertically into the sea, making a most wonderful sight and an enormous splash. Everything seemed to have cleared off, so I circled round the two Huns. They took an awful long time to come down on land and I watched the army rush up and capture them."

The rear gunner of a Junkers Ju.88 "landed one plumb in the middle of my windscreen, splintering it in all directions and making it quite opaque" after which he could only be an observer of a combat that continued from the Blackmore Vale to Poole where a colleague, Sergeant Pilot Bill Kearsey, finished it off [14 November 1940].

Marrs avenged the death of a comrade, Pilot Officer A.R. Watson, by creeping up behind the culprit Messerschmitt Bf.109, in its blind spot, to send it flaming into the sea in "the easiest victory I've had" [28 November 1940].

The next was much the same. The target was a single German aircraft that was reportedly entering the Middle Wallop sector [4 January 1941]. Marrs found the Dornier Do.17 above Ringstead Bay and came at it from the sea as it "turned south and dived like stink for the clouds". That was too late as Spitfire R6968 raked it with fire from 400 yards, closing to 250 yards, silencing return fire and setting the engines on fire. It was seen to splash into the sea five miles south-east of Portland Bill. No one survived.

Marrs had an amazingly lucky escape when a bomb crashed through his room at RAF Warmwell [1 April 1941]. He was not there at the time because he was having the Distinguished Flying Cross pinned on his uniform in Buckingham Palace by King George VI.

Celebrated his twentieth birthday [10 July 1941]. Flew to Brest in one of the first long-range offensive missions to be undertaken by the station, which provided fighter escort for 18 Hampden bombers of 44 Squadron and 114 Squadron, in a daylight raid on its German capital ships [24 July 1941]. Marrs was killed by German flak, bringing true a Warmwell prophecy that no German fighter pilot was going to take the "Boy".

His body was recovered and is in the military cemetery at Brest.

McArdle — Bournemouth's first pilot **William McArdle** [born 1875] supplied motor cars to royalty and entrepreneurs from his Motor Mac's garage in Holdenhurst Road. Taught to fly by Louis Bleriot, he became a passionate flying enthusiast, selling the "FINEST GARAGE IN ENGLAND" and moving to France [1909] where he built a shed beside that of aviator Henri Farman at Chalons Camp, near Paris.

McArdle then entered into a partnership with rich flyer J. Armstrong Drexel, son of a Philadelphia banker, and returned to England for aviation meetings including the famous Southbourne event. He also ventured into the countryside, as is proved by a postcard showing his monoplane "pitched in a field just opposite" the sender's house near Fordingbridge [19 July 1910].

McKeown — veteran navy flyer **Captain David "Paddy" McKeown** [retired 1977] was the commander of HMS Osprey, the Portland shore base. His 35 years flying service for the Royal Navy had taken him up in 52 different types of aircraft, for a total of 4,500 hours airborne, and involved 800 deck landings on sixteen aircraft carriers. He had survived a mid-air collision in a "Corsair" over southern India in 1945. He was mentioned in despatches when flying a Sea Fury from HMS *Ocean* in the Korean War, and again whilst flying Sea Hawks from HMS *Albion* at Suez [1956].

McNamara — American flyer **Ensign J.F. McNamara**, operating from Portland Royal Naval Air Station, became the first United States aviatior to attack a submarine in an "apparently successful" engagement of a German U-boat [1917].

Meyrick Park Airfield — used by visiting air display pilots, such as Gustav Hamel, and notable as the only Bournemouth aerodrome that has survived under grass. The early pilots used the cricket pitch that is overlooked by the pavilion (Ordnance Survey map reference SZ 084 922).

Miller — Spitfire flyer **Pilot Officer Rogers Freeman Garland "Mick" Miller** [1920-40] of 609 Squadron at RAF Warmwell claimed half a Dornier kill [13 July 1940]. He would be killed when his fighter collided with a Messerschmitt Bf.110 (3U+FT) at 24,000 feet above Bellamy's Farm, Piddletrenthide [27 September 1940]. The Spitfire crashed on the Cheselbourne side of the parish boundary. Miller is buried in St Nicholas' churchyard, Radford Semele, Warwickshire.

Mitchell — Spitfire flyer **Pilot Officer Gordon Thomas Manners Mitchell** [1910-40] of 609 Squadron from RAF Warmwell was shot down, in L1095, as the Luftwaffe attacked a convoy off Portland [11 July 1940]. His body was later washed up on the Isle of Wight and he is buried at All Saints churchyard, Letchworth, Hertfordshire.

MOHD — squadron code of 644 Squadron, flying Halifax tug-planes from RAF Tarrant Rushton [1943-44].

Moortown Aerodrome — private airfield at Canford Magna, near Poole, used by Captain the Right Honourable Freddie Guest of Canford House.

He established it when he was appointed Secretary of State for Air [1921] and it continued in use into the 1930s, when he was a Squadron Leader in the Royal Auxiliary Air Force.

Moreton Admiralty Airship Station — established on 355 acres of requisitioned land between the Dorchester to Wareham railway line and the hamlet around Woodsford Castle (Ordnance Survey map reference SY 760 895), in the final year of the Great War [1918].

Buildings were constructed, including airship sheds, gas holders, and repair worksheds. The site was entirely in the parish of Woodsford rather than Moreton but was named for the nearby Moreton Station, to the south-east and opposite the Frampton Arms.

The signing of the Armistice [11 November 1918] caused an immediate halt to the work and no airship ever landed operationally. That said, it has left its mark on the ground, including an access road westwards from Higher Woodsford hamlet and several buildings.

Indeed the site is better preserved than the later Warmwell Aerodrome, on the other side of the railway track, and aviation historians have sometimes confused the two.

Mosquito — parts for wartime de Havilland Mosquitoes, famous for their pathfinding flare-dropping and precision bombing raids, were made by the Airspeed factory at Somerford, Christchurch [1943-44]. Airspeed was owned by de Havilland, though it operated at that time under its own name.

Leslie Dawson, writing in *Wings over Dorset*, states that "over a hundred" Mosquitoes were built at Christchurch, — 122 actually — though this fact has not filtered through to the lengthy production placename list displayed at the RAF Museum, in Hendon.

The "Wooden Wonder" continued to be seen in Dorset skies, as Leslie Dawson goes on to record and I can also recall from my childhood. Two night-fighter variants were flown by Flight Refuelling Limited, then at Tarrant Rushton Aerodrome, and their registrations are given as G-ALGU and G-ALGV. Airwork Services operated several.

Three Mark XVIs were overhauled at Hurn, Dawson adds, on being sold to the Israeli Air Force at the time of the Suez crisis [1956]. "Two Christchurch-built Mosquitoes survived into the late 1980s," he concludes.

Others with local associations had by this time ended their days in bonfires, either as acts of deliberate destruction or vandalism — or indeed both — during a series of incidents around Hurn's sprawling perimeter.

MW — code letters of 217 Squadron, flying Avro Ansons on coastal patrols from RAF Warmwell at the beginning of the Second World War.

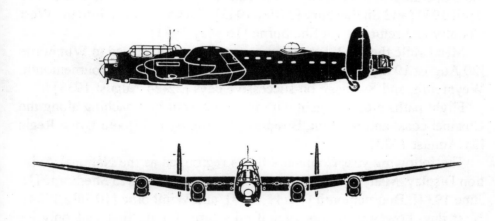

Lancaster: Bomber Command 'strays'
occasionally landed at RAF Hurn
and Tarrant Rushton – lost, damaged,
or diverted

N

National Aviation Displays — Sir Alan Cobham's Flying Circus began its first tour at Hanworth [12 April 1932]. Display days number 122 and 123 reached Bournemouth [12-13 August 1932] with Weymouth chosen for the following day.

Smaller towns did better in the following year's schedules when two tours operated simultaneouly. No.2 Tour dropped in on Christchurch [30 April 1933] and Shaftesbury [2 May 1933]. They went deep into the West Country and returned via Sherborne [16 May 1933].

Meanwhile the No.1 Tour were approaching and arrived in Wimborne [20 August 1933]. Petworth, Sussex, was next. Then came Bournemouth, Weymouth, and Swanage on successive days [22-24 August 1933].

Flight paths crossed again with the No.2 Tour approaching along the Channel coast and reaching Bridport [28 August 1933] and Lyme Regis [31 August 1933].

The following year Cobham's flyers regrouped as the National Aviation Display. Many of its calls were return visits, such as to Sherborne [15 June 1934], Bournemouth [7 July 1934], and Wimborne [10 July 1934]. Next day, however, it was Blandford's turn, for its first and only air display. There were more return venues the following month, including Lyme Regis [10 August 1934] and Swanage [14 August 1934].

Flying held its grasp on the popular imagination throughout the next spring and summer. Dorset skies saw Cobham's armada again, around Yeovil [1 June 1935], and then the team was split into the Astra Show and the Ferry Show. The former visited Bournemouth [6 July 1935], Christchurch [10 August 1935], Swanage [15 August 1935], Weymouth [16 August 1935], Lyme Regis [19 August 1935], and Wimborne [31 August 1935].

Meantime the Ferry Show also came to Dorset — whilst their comrades were over Swanage — with a visit to Gillingham in Dorset, rather than Kent, as the previous day they had been in Glastonbury and the following day it was Crewkerne's turn.

Naylor — Canadian flyer **Pilot Officer Naylor** of 418 (City of Edmonton) Squadron was killed when a Mosquito fighter-bomber crashed at Alder Road, Poole [23 July 1944].

Necker Island — 75-acres of the Caribbean, two miles off Virgin Gorda in the British Virgin Islands, owned by Lord Cobham, the founder of Flight Refuelling Limited, who sold it to Richard Branson of Virgin Airways for £300,000 [1979].

New Zealand heroes — fighter pilots Squadron Leader Terence Lovell-Gregg and Pilot Officer Cecil Hight were shot down and killed by the Luftwaffe, minutes from each other, in separate Battle of Britain dog-fights over opposite ends of the Dorset coast [18.00 hours, 15 August 1940]. Lovell-Gregg's Hurricane came down at Abbotsbury and Hight's Spitfire fell on Bournemouth.

Lovell-Gregg was from Marlborough, New Zealand, and Hight lived at Stratford, on the other side of the Cook Strait, in North Island.

Nichols — Hurricane flyer **Pilot Officer Dennis Nichols** [born 1921] of 56 Squadron, from RAF Boscombe Down, was shot down at Alton Pancras whilst on his first combat sortie [7 October 1940]. He parachuted clear of the stricken fighter but had a hard landing and was taken to Dorchester Hospital with a suspected fractured spine.

9U — squadron code of 644 Squadron, flying Halifax tug-planes for airborne forces, from RAF Hurn [1943-44].

NK — squadron code of 118 Squadron, flying Spitfires from RAF Warmwell [9-18 April 1941].

Norman - captain of industry **Sir Arthur Norman** [born 1917], won the Distinguished Flying Cross and bar [1943-44]. He lived at Manston House and retired to Gale Cottage, Hammoon.

Nowierski — Polish Spitfire flyer **Pilot Officer Tadeusz Nowierski** [died 1983] of 609 Squadron from RAF Warmwell put a Messerschmitt Bf.109 escort fighter into the sea off Weymouth during the Luftwaffe's Adlertag (Eagle Day) attack [13 August 1940]. He parachuted out of Spitfire N3223, on to Salisbury Plain, when his undercarriage failed [5 October 1940].

Claimed a Messerschmitt Bf.109 destroyed [10 October 1940] and half shares in the kills of a Messerschmitt Bf.110 and a Dornier Do.17 [both 2 December 1940].

Became Polish Liaison Officer to Headquarters, 11 Group Fighter Command [1942] and would be promoted to Group Captain, commanding RAF Dunholme Lodge. Returned to Poland [1947].

NX — squadron code of 131 (County of Kent) Squadron, flying Spitfires on bomber escort duties from RAF Hurn [10-14 July 1943].

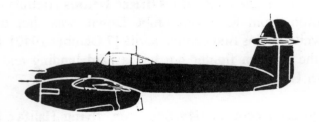

**Whirlwind: Yeovil-made, by Westland
Aircraft Limited, it operated in the
mid-war period from RAF Warmwell – including
the named 'Bellows' – as an escort fighter,
flown by Canadian and other Dominion
and Empire pilots**

O

O'Brien — Spitfire flyer **Pilot Officer Peter O'Brien** from RAF Warmwell claimed a third share of 152 Squadron's kill of a Heinkel He.111 bomber off Portland [15 September 1940]. It probably belonged to Kampfgruppe 55 from Chartres.

He also scored a third share in the kill of a Junkers Ju.88 that was shot down at Ladywell Barn, Imber, Wiltshire [17 September 1940]. His was the only Spitfire of Blue Section that avoided the bomber's return fire and did not have to crash-land.

Oborne crash — of a German bomber into the hillside below Oborne Wood, east of Sherborne [7 May 1941]. The pilot baled out but the other three members of the crew died in the wreckage. They were buried in Oborne churchyard, until removal of the remains by the Volksbund, to the German war cemetery, Cannock Chase, Staffordshire [1963].

Okeford Fitzpaine crash — of Hurricane N2434 belonging to 56 Squadron from RAF Boscombe Down, on the day the Luftwaffe blitzed Sherborne [30 September 1940]. The pilot parachuted safely.

Olenski — Polish Spitfire pilot **Flying Officer Zbigniew Olenski** [1907-70] flew with 234 Squadron from RAF Warmwell [5 September 1940]. He already had combat experience — having claimed a probable Messerschmitt Bf.109 kill and a definite Bf.110 destruction — which, coupled with a Warsaw aeronautical engineering background, enabled him to suggest modifications to the Mark I Spitfire.

This report, which was adopted, led to his move to the Aerodynamics Department of the Royal Aircraft Establishment, Farnborough [28 March 1941]. After the war, on being released from the RAF as a Flight-Lieutenant, he worked for aircraft manufacturers A. V. Roe in Manchester, as an aerodynamicist, and played his part in the creating of the most beautiful aerodynamics of the century — the Avro Vulcan.

1-11 — the "One Eleven" airliner, made by the British Aircraft Corporation, merged into British Aerospace plc, at their works beside Hurn (Bournemouth) Airport [1963-84].

A BAC 1-11 Series 510 airliner, G-AVMO, was flown to Cosford, Shropshire, to join the British Airways collection in the Aerospace Museum [29 December 1992].

Openshaw — test pilot of Westland Aircraft Limited **Major Laurence Openshaw** was killed in a collision at Ensbury Park Aerodrome, Bournemouth [6 June 1927]. His Westland Widgeon was flying at low-level in a competitive event.

HMS Osprey — Portland Royal Naval Air Station, as it was commissioned for the Air Anti-Submarine Warfare School [24 April 1959].

Owermoigne crashes — Westland Wallace K6057 of 6 Air Training Corps crashed near the hamlet of Holworth, midway between Owermoigne village and the sea [14 January 1938].

A wartime German crash was, apparently, a Messerschmitt Bf.110 fighter-bomber of Zerstörergeschwader 26 which had been involved in the attack on the Westland Aircraft factory at Yeovil [7 October 1940]. It was claimed by Spitfires of 609 Squadron from RAF Warmwell.

Spitfire P8516, a Mark II fighter of 118 Squadron, flew into hills south of the village [4 August 1941].

Oxford — twin-engined advanced trainer produced for the RAF by Airspeed (1934) Limited at its factory in Somerford, Christchurch, and elsewhere. A total of 4,411 were made by the company [1938-45] but taking those from other factories into account the grand total would exceed 8,000.

P

Pamphill crash — into Kingston Lacy Park 200 yards north-north-east of Kingston Lacy House, of Halifax bomber DT684 of 58 Squadron from RAF Holmsley South, Hampshire [24 January 1943]. It was on a transit flight to Talbenny, Haverfordwest, and suffered engine failure shortly after its 13.30 hours take-off.

The crew were killed: Flying Officer M.A. Legg of the Royal New Zealand Air Force (aged 32); Flying Officer G.R. Pringle, a Royal Canadian Air Force air observer (29); and Warrant Officers L.E. Gilpin (21) and S.J. Prince (25) also of the RCAF, who were wireless operators and gunners. They are buried in Bransgore churchyard, in the New Forest.

Paraguay — an ex-BOAC Mark V Sunderland flying-boat from Poole, converted into a Sandringham-3 for carrying 21 passengers and sold to the Argentine airline Dodero [November 1945].

Pegasus bridge — the Orne canal bridge in Normandy, midway between the D-Day beach-heads and the strategic inland town of Caen, was the first objectives in northern France to be captured during the invasion of Europe [01.30 hours, 6 June 1944]. Operation Coup de Main, this surprise attack, was carried out by Major John Howard with "D" company of the 2nd Battalion, Oxford and Buckinghamshire Light Infantry, one of six gliders of the 6th Airborne Division that had lifted off from RAF Tarrant Rushton [22.56 hours, 5 June 1944], towed by Halifax tug-planes.

The canal bridge would henceforth be known as Pegasus Bridge, from the division's emblem, and the nearby swingbridge over the River Orne became Horsa Bridge, from the men's gliders.

Penrose — aviator **Harald Penrose** [born 1904] of Stallen at Nether Compton was the first person to fly higher than the highest point on earth. Repeating the exercise, on the morning of 26 January 1933 as test pilot of the Westland Aircraft Works, he took the Houston-Westland aeroplane to

a record 35,000 feet over Poole Bay. Air-Commodore P.F.M. Fellowes
was in the observer's cockpit. It proved the feasibility of what became,
later that year, the first successful flight over Mount Everest, with
Commodore and Mrs Fellowes leading the three small aircraft in a Puss
Moth. Their exploits enthralled picture house audiences in the film *Wings
over Everest*.

As for the first day at 35,000 feet, the flight began at Yeovil at 10.10
am into a 20 mph north-west wind. The aircraft was at its full weight of
4,870 lb and Penrose took her south to south-east to Weymouth Bay and
the Purbeck coast.

Maximum altitude was reached at 11.24 over Poole Bay, with the
temperature at 76 degrees Fahrenheit below zero, the engine's performance (550 horsepower at its normal ceiling of 11,500 feet) reduced to
an estimated 150 horsepower, and a speed for a few moments of 140 mph.
The wind at that height was thought to be about 50 miles an hour.

"My chief concern was whether the controls would operate at such a
high altitude," Penrose said after returning to Yeovil at noon, "They
worked perfectly, and I was able to demonstrate by working the controls
that complete mastery of the machine was maintained. Although I had ice
forming over some of my instruments and the control panel and over
my face mask and goggle mask, I was perfectly warm owing to my
electrically-heated clothing and equipment. As a matter of fact I actually
had my goggles more often off than on, because I was so warm."

Earlier in the week, there had been another test, Commodore Fellowes
said, and he found that he had to replace his fountain pen with a pencil,
because the low pressure at high altitude caused the ink to burst out at the
nib.

Penrose told Rodney Legg in 1970 that before taking Fellowes into the
upper atmosphere he had tried out the aeroplane himself. That time, when
alone he topped an estimated 30,000 feet and became the first to fly
higher than the earth, the engine cut out. It had frozen up and he entered
into a long glide back to earth, but succeeded in re-starting it as he
dropped through the clouds at about 8,000 feet. The cause was a simple
icing problem that was cured by adaptations to the fuel pipe and its
lagging. He also realised his altimeter was unreliable at great heights (the

35,000 feet of the record being a later ground re-calculation of what the instruments showed at the time as being 38,900 feet).

Over the next two decades, Penrose tested and flew more than 400 types and variations in design of British and foreign aircraft. In the process he returned to his original job as a designer-technician to make major contributions in the development of rotor craft and devising what became the standard system of cabin pressurisation.

On retirement [1968] he embarked on a six volume history of British aviation from 1903 to the Second World War.

Peto seaplane — built by George Parnall and Company at Bristol and housed in a hangar built beside the conning tower of big Royal Navy submarine M2 [launched 1919] which was recommissioned as an aircraft-carrier [1927]. She had a 28-feet wing-span that folded to only eight feet. Experimental flights achieved a maximum speed of 113 miles per hour and endurance times of two hours in the air. What seemed like hopeful progress came to an abrupt halt off Dorset, three miles west of Portland Bill, when the submarine dived with its hangar doors open (or faulty), letting in the sea [10.30 hours, 26 January 1932].

She sank to 17 fathoms and the entire crew of 60 submariners — including Peto's pilot and ten men who operated the doors — were drowned. The tiny seaplane was later raised but out of respect for the dead it was decided that she should be scrapped, and the project died with her. Salvage attempts to lift the huge submarine were eventually abandoned [8 September 1932] and she was left as a tomb. Divers say the 305-feet hull is still intact, perhaps because it sits on sand, and that the hangar doors remain open.

Phoenix — pilotless rocket-boosted battlefield reconnaissance spy-plane and launcher developed by Flight Refuelling Limited at Wimborne [1980s].

Piddlehinton crash — a Spitfire of 609 Squadron from RAF Warmwell crash-landed near the village when its pilot was blinded by glycol fumes after the cooling system of the fighter's Merlin engine had been punctured by gunfire during a Battle of Britain dog-fight [26 July 1940].

Piddletrenthide crashes — of a Messerschmitt Bf.110 (3U+FT) belonging to Zerstörergeschwader 26, the Geschwader named Horst Wessel after the Nazi writer of a militant anti-Semitic song which became a national anthem. It was in collision with Pilot Officer Mick Miller's Spitfire of 609 Squadron from RAF Warmwell [27 September 1940].

The German pilot, Georg Jackstedt, parachuted into captivity, but his wireless operator, Emil Lidtke, was killed. The collision occurred at 24,000 feet above Bellamy's Farm and the aircraft crashed beside its boundary hedge with Dole's Ash Farm. It had been taking part in an abortive raid on the Parnall Aircraft Company at Yate, near Chipping Sodbury.

Miller's Spitfire came down on the Cheselbourne side of the parish boundary.

Pimperne crash — at Nutford Farm, north of Blandford, of a Dornier Do.17 reconnaissance aircraft (5F+OM) the crew of which survived and had their injuries tended in the farmhouse [21 July 1940]. The kill was claimed by Hurricanes of 238 Squadron from RAF Middle Wallop.

***Plymouth* class** — Sandringham Mark 5 flying-boats operating from Poole Harbour by British Overseas Airways, on middle-distance routes to the Gulf and India, and onwards to Malaya and Hong Kong [1947-48]. Carrying 22 passengers each, the Poole fleet comprised nine boats: *Pembroke, Penzance, Perth, Pevensey, Poole, Portland, Portmarnock, Portsea,* and *Portsmouth.*

PN — squadron code of 41 Squadron, flying Spitfires from RAF Warmwell [7-18 March 1945].

Pollock — Hurricane pilot **Flight Lieutenant Norval E. Pollock** of 439 (Royal Canadian Air Force) Squadron was killed near RAF Hurn when his Hurricane LD972 collided with an American P-47 Thunderbolt from USAAF Christchurch [21 March 1944].

Pooch - bull terrier **Pilot Officer Pooch** was the mascot of 152 Squadron at RAF Warmwell [1940-41].

RAF Poole — as it was known for just one week, being re-named RAF Hamworthy before the arrival of its first military flying-boats [October 1942].

Poole crashes — one of the returning Heinkel He.111 bombers that had devastated the Bristol Aeroplane Company's works at Filton during the Battle of Britain [25 September 1940] was shot down over Poole. Belonging to Kampfgeschwader 55, the bomber (G1+LR) ploughed into Underwood, Westminster Road, Branksome Park. The five crew were killed. This kill was claimed by Hurricanes of 238 Squadron from RAF Middle Wallop.

Sergeant Pilot Bill Kearsey finished off a Junkers Ju.88 bomber which Pilot Officer Eric "Boy" Marrs had engaged over the Blackmore Vale [14 November 1940]. It came down as a fireball, exploding fifty feet from a cobbler's shed, near the corner of Ringwood Road and Herbert Avenue.

A Mosquito of 418 (City of Edmonton) Squadron, from RAF Hurn, crashed 200 yards west of Alder Road Drill Hall, Upper Parkstone [23 July 1944]. It had apparently clipped the roof of a building in Mossley Avenue, during a low-level daylight flight, and exploded shortly after hitting the ground. Pilot Officer Bowhay and Naylor were killed.

Poole Harbour crashes — a Messerschmitt Bf.109 escort fighter was shot down during the Luftwaffe's Adlertag (Eagle Day) attack [13 August 1940]. The pilot, Unteroffizier Wilhelm Hohenseldt, was rescued and made prisoner of war. Pilot Officer Crook, in a Spitfire of 609 Squadron from RAF Warmwell, claimed the kill.

Hurricane P3599 of 238 Squadron was shot down off Poole [1 October 1940]. The squadron then also lost Hurricane P3984 in a Battle of Britain dog-fight over the same spot [10 October 1940]. Though wounded, Pilot Officer Bob Doe, parachuted to a soft landing in "the sewage lagoon" on Brownsea Island, and his fighter sped on into the Isle of Purbeck where it crashed below Corfe Castle.

BOAC flying-boat *Hailsham*, returning from Singapore, found the English coast obscured by fog [4 March 1946]. She managed to find the main water-runway "Trot" in Poole Harbour but then veered sideways and damaged her floats in the shallows beside Brownsea Island. No one was hurt but *Hailsham* was inundated by rising tide. She was later pulled clear but only to be towed away for scrap.

Portesham crash — a Junkers Ju.87 "Stuka" dive-bomber was shot down between the village and Rodden during the Luftwaffe's routed Adlertag (Eagle Day) attack [13 August 1940]. The kill was claimed by Flight-Lieutenant Derek Boitel-Gill in a Spitfire of 152 Squadron from RAF Warmwell. The dive-bomber was one of those targeted on Middle Wallop Aerodrome, Hampshire.

Portland crashes — a Junkers Ju.88 (B3+DC) was brought down, almost undamaged, in a crash-landing at "The Castles" clifftop beside Blacknor Fort [11 August 1940]. Claimed by a Hurricane of 213 Squadron from RAF Exeter, its "B3" markings indicated it belonged to Kampfgeschwader 54, a bomber wing whose death's head emblem — Totenkopf — appeared on the fuselage just aft of the transparent nose.

The sea off Portland saw numerous casualties through the Battle of Britain and for almost the duration of the Second World War. Most of the aircraft belonged to the Luftwaffe but they were joined by many defending Spitfires and Hurricanes.

The following losses were inflicted on the Royal Air Force over the sea off Portland in Battle of Britain dog-fights:

Spitfire of 609 Squadron [9 July 1940].

Spitfires L1069 and L1095 of 609 Squadron and Hurricane N2485 of 501 Squadron [11 July 1940].

Hurricane P3084 of 501 Squadron [12 July 1940].

Spitfire K9901 of 152 Squadron [25 July 1940].

Hurricanes L2057, P3783, P3885, and R4092 of 601 Squadron [11 August 1940].

Hurricanes P3348 of 213 Squadron and P3177 of 238 Squadron [13 August 1940].

Hurricanes P2872 and P3215 of 87 Squadron [15 August 1940].

Hurricanes N2646, P2766, and P3200 of 213 Squadron, and Spitfire R6810 of 152 Squadron [25 August 1940].

Spitfire R6831 of 152 Squadron [27 August 1940].

Hurricanes P3655 and P3088 of 56 Squadron, and Spitfire L1072 of 152 Squadron [30 September 1940].

Hurricane P3421 of 56 Squadron [10 October 1940].

The following fighters were also shot down off the Dorset coast after interceptions that began over Portland:

Spitfire R6614 of 152 Squadron and Hurricane R4097 of 238 Squadron [11 August 1940].

Spitfire R6985 of 234 Squadron [15 August 1940].

German losses into the English Channel are recorded with less accuracy but the following, at least, were seen from Portland:

Junkers Ju.87 [9 July 1940].

Heinkel He.111 [15 September 1940].

Dornier Do.17 [4 January 1941].

A Royal Navy Whirlwind helicopter crashed at Portland [9 October 1968].

Another ditched in the sea at Portland Harbour [20 June 1969].

Three were killed and four saved when a Royal Navy Wessex helicopter crashed in the sea off Portland during a photographic reconnaissance exercise [20 May 1971].

The next helicopter to ditch in the sea was a Royal Navy Sea King [13 January 1972], followed a month later by a Navy Wessex, also off Portland [16 February 1972].

Portland Royal Naval Air Station — established on The Mere marshes in the corner of Portland Harbour between the Chesil Beach and Portland Castle, for float-planes during the Great War [26 September 1916]. Initially designated HMS Sereptia. Expansion followed, including a seaplane shed, and the lagoon beside the oil tanks became the home-base for the 12 Short and Wright float-planes of No.416 and 417 Flights, comprising 241 Squadron [1918].

Extension of this into the vast acreage of modern concrete and tarmac (Ordnance Survey map reference SY 682 743) is much more recent. Quarry waste was not dumped across the entirety of The Mere until the middle of the Cold War [1959].

Renamed HMS Osprey [24 April 1959].

Posener — South African volunteer **Pilot Officer Frederick Hyam Posener** [1917-40], flying Spitfire K9880 of 152 Squadron from RAF Warmwell, was shot down off Swanage in a Battle of Britain dog-fight [20 July 1940]. It was his second operational sortie. He was one of only 21 South African pilots who took part in the battle.

Powell — Malmesbury's Member of Parliament **Walter Powell** was whisked away into the sky, never to be seen again, from Cliff Close, Eype, Symondsbury [10 December 1881]. The War Office hot-air balloon *Saladin*, on secondment to the Meteorological Society, was the cause of the misadventure. Its remains, though without those of the MP, were discovered on the slopes of Sierra del Piedroza in the mountains of Spain [20 January 1882].

Powerstock Admiralty Airship Station — as it was sometimes called, being above Gray's Farm in this parish, is listed here under its official designation as Toller Admiralty Airship Station.

Powerstock crash — of Wellington X9785 belonging to 218 Squadron from RAF Marham, Norfolk, which had been on a mission to bomb German capital ships in the French Atlantic port of Brest [16 December 1941]. Five of the crew baled out over Chilfrome and the pilot, Sergeant Vezina, successfully brought his crippled aircraft to a crash-landing at Holm Farm, above West Milton. The starboard engine had failed.

PR — code letters of 609 (West Riding) Squadron flying Spitfires from RAF Warmwell [1940-41].

Proud — pre-war pilot **Group Captain Harold John Granville Ellis Proud** [born 1906] joined the RAF in 1924. He became station commander of RAF Hurn for 38 Wing Army Co-operation Command, providing transport support for the 1st Airborne Division [1942-43]. Reached the rank of Air Commodore and commanded the Far East Base, Singapore [1949-51].

Puddletown crash — Miles Master N7551 of the Central Gunnery School, flying from RAF Warmwell, was abandoned out of control over Puddletown Heath [22 April 1940].

Pytlak — Hurricane flyer **Pilot Officer T.W. Pytlak** of 302 (Poznanski) Squadron at RAF Warmwell was killed in a flying accident [9 September 1941]. The Polish Squadron had arrived at the station four days earlier. He was aged 22 and is buried in the RAF plot at Warmwell churchyard.

Dakota: ubiquitous transport aircraft of
the latter half of the Second World War and
for years to come, the C-47 ferried casualties
from the 'Battle of the Bulge' in the
Ardennes to RAF Tarrant Rushton – and hospital at
Blandford Camp – after the last Christmas of the war

Q

Qantas Empire Airways — the Australian airline, took delivery of *Coogee, Coorong,* and *Corio* from the Imperial Airways C-class fleet of Empire flying-boats that were being dispersed from Southamptom Water to Poole Harbour [1939]. *Coorong* and *Corio* would later be exchanged for ex-Poole flying-boat *Calypso* and *Centaurus.*

Back in Europe, *Coorong* joined sister flying-boat *Cambria*, from the Poole fleet in evacuating 469 of the 30,000 British, Australian, and New Zealand troops garrisoning the island of Crete, in the teeth of German airborne invasion [May 1941]. Thirteen flights were made across the Mediterranean, from Suda Bay to Alexandria.

Quantas is the acronym of the Queensland and Northern Territory Aerial Service, which is the airline of the Australian Commonwealth. Its links with Hurn and BOAC led to a joint service between Britain and Australia, which resumed when the war in Europe ended.

Lancastrian G-AGLV of British Overseas Airways Corporation lifted off from Hurn in the inaugural flight, via Lydda in British Palestine (now Lod, Israel) and Karachi in British India (now in Pakistan), for Sydney, Australia. Of eleven seats, only six were occupied for the 12,000 mile flight which which became the world's longest post-war scheduled service [30 May 1945].

QV — squadron code of 19 Squadron, flying Spitfires from RAF Warmwell [1-14 June 1942].

R

RAK — squadron code of 604 (County of Middlesex) Squadron, flying Mosquito night-fighters from RAF Hurn [3 May - 13 July 1944].

Rayment — Blenheim pilot **Flight-Lieutenant Douglas Rayment** of the Special Duties Flight from RAF Christchurch was lost at sea, 33 miles south of St Alban's Head [17 July 1941]. He had told his gunner, Sergeant R. Sadler, to fire at a mystery object, thought to be a weather balloon, floating in the water: "There you are, have a go. You can't miss!" Two bursts of machine-gun fire followed and the aircraft's wireless then went dead. No one ever knew what happened.

RB — squadron code of 66 Squadron, flying Spitfires on bomber escort duties from RAF Hurn [10-14 July 1943].

Rebbeck — Bournemouth-born **Rear-Admiral Sir Edward Rebbeck** [born 1901] served in the Great war in HMS *Erin*, and in the Second World War in HMS *Birmingham*, before making his mark on naval aviation. He was Commanding Officer to Anthorn Royal Naval Air Station [1946], ADC to the Queen [1952], and Rear-Admiral Reserve Aircraft, up to retirement [1952-55]. Then he spent a decade working for the Vickers Group.

Reddington — Spitfire flyer **Sergeant Pilot Leslie Arthur Edwin Reddington** [1914-40] of 152 Squadron from RAF Warmwell was shot down into the sea on the day that the Luftwaffe blitzed Sherborne [30 September 1940]. His fighter, L1072, crashed into the sea. Reddington's body was not recovered but his widow was pregnant in Coventry with their second daughter; Lesley Reddington was born in February 1941.

Rhodes-Moorhouse — first flyer to win the Victoria Cross "**William Barnard Rhodes-Moorhouse** VC, RFC, DIED APRIL 27th 1915 AT MERVILLE, FRANCE, FROM WOUNDS RECEIVED IN BOMBING COURTRAI, AGED 27 YEARS. IN SACRED LOVING MEMORY. PER ARDUA AD ASTRA." The inscriptions in a railed plot overlooking Parnham House and Beaminster gloss over the superlative. He had provided the Royal Flying Corps with its first Victoria Cross.

He had taken off at 15.00 hours on 26 April 1915 in a BE 2b biplane, from Merville, to drop a hundred pound bomb on a railway bridge over the River Lys at Courtrai in German-occupied Belgium. To do so he flew at three hundred feet through a hail of bullets, mainly unleashed from the church belfry, and the bomb hit its target — temporarily tearing up the track. Rhodes-Moorhouse and the BE 2b were equally shot-up but limped back together to Merville. There the flyer was resigned to his fate, with massive gunshot wounds to his thigh and abdomen.

"I am not a brave man," he told the chaplain, "but I have tried to do my duty." He survived only 24 hours.

Such was the admiration of his commanding officer that he implemented William's request that his body should be shipped home to Dorset — itself a rare honour as it was a wish denied to almost all the other dead heroes.

William has another claim to fame — in the carefree days of pre-war aviation he had been the first to fly through the Golden Gate at San Francisco.

Parnham House had been bought by his Maori mother in 1913. There he left a widow, Linda, and a baby son, William Henry Rhodes-Moorhouse [1914-40] who would follow his father's example in the next war and win a Distinguished Flying Cross for 601 (County of London) Squadron in the Battle of Britain. At its close, on 6 September 1940, his Hurricane was shot down near Tonbridge, Kent. His ashes were returned to the Parnham plot. Linda had now lost both her husband and her son — at the same ages and from the same cause.

Ridgeway crash — precise parish not known, of a belly-landed Heinkel He.111 H-8 bomber [5 April 1941]. The crew were unhurt and taken prisoner. They had been attacking Channel shipping and ended up in Dorset through a navigational error.

Robinson—Spitfire flyer **Sergeant Pilot Denis Norman Robinson** of 152 Squadron from RAF Warmwell crashed at Bestwall, Wareham, after a Battle of Britain dog-fight over Swanage [8 August 1940]. He had a remarkable escape—the fuselage of K9894 ended up standing vertically, with the propeller embedded in the meadow, and he was able to jump down on the grass.

He had claimed a Messerschmitt Bf.109 in the first week of that busy month [5 August 1940], and returned to the sky to account for another [15 August 1940]. He then had a Junkers Ju.87 [17 August 1940] and finally a Junkers Ju.88 [4 September 1940] before being posted to RAF Upavon, Wiltshire [26 September 1940].

Robinson survived the war and became a civilian pilot [1946-78].

Robinson—former Hurricane pilot **Squadron Leader Michael Lister Robinson** [1917-42] left 238 Squadron at RAF Chilbolton, from which he had been defending the Dorset coast, to take charge of Spitfires of 609 Squadron at RAF Warmwell [4 October 1940]. He came with several Messerschmitt claims and would share in two more Bf.110s within days, during the attack on the Westland Aircraft Company at Yeovil [7 October 1940].

Eight more Messerschmitts, Bf.109s, were claimed in a rapid tally of kills, plus one probable destruction [8 May - 24 July 1941]. Robinson was then gazetted with the Distinguished Service Order [5 August 1941] and posted to Biggin Hill.

It was as leader of Tangmere Wing, heading 340 Squadron, that he failed to return from a sweep along the English Channel [10 April 1942]. Michael Robinson was the son of Sir Roy Robinson [1883-1952], chairman of the Forestry Commission, who was created first Baron Robinson of Kielder Forest [1947].

Roe—pioneer aviator **Humphrey Verdon Roe** [1878-1949], second husband of contraception advocate Dr Marie Stopes, lived at the Higher Lighthouse, Portland.

His *Who's Who* entry explains how he came to make flying machines: "From 1909 onwards, when flying seemed to be a dream, his foresight and faith in its future led him to devote the whole of his capital and talents to helping his brother Sir Alliott Verdon-Roe, to establish the Avro biplane."

They founded plane-makers A.V. Roe and Company Limited. Humphrey left in 1917 to join the Royal Flying Corps, in France, and was wounded on active service [1918].

Rolls — pioneer automobile manufacturer and aviator, the **Honourable Charles Stewart Rolls** [1877-1910] was the first Briton to be killed in an aeroplane crash. His biplane stalled in an air-display at Southbourne, Bournemouth [12 July 1910]. The accident is commemorated by a plaque in the grounds of St Peter's School, in St Catherine's Road.

Royal Naval Air Landing Ship 50 — the vessel in Portland Harbour with more helicopter landings to her credit than any other vessel in the Royal Navy or, perhaps anywhere in the world. Now at 100,000 drops and rising.

Royal Navy Seaplane School — moved from Calshot on Southampton Water to Sandbanks, beside Poole Harbour [15 May 1940].

Seafire: Fleet Air Arm version of the famous Spitfire, with all-round vision and folding wings for use on aircraft-carriers, converted by Airspeed Limited at Christchurch Aerodrome and flown from Henstridge Royal Naval Air Station

S

Saladin — War Office hot-air balloon 60 feet high and 30 feet across, made at the Royal Gun Factory, Woolwich Arsenal [1878], last seen on the Dorset coast, above Symondsbury and then disappearing across Lyme Bay [16.15 hours, 10 December 1881].

The ill-fated flight began from Bath [14.00 hours] and was carrying out cloud measurements of temperature and water-vapour for the Meteorological Society. The occupants underestimated the northerly wind and the perilous implications of their seaward flight-path.

The balloon clipped a clifftop pasture at Cliff Close, Eype's Mouth, throwing two of the occupants clear as well as much-needed ballast. Captain James Templer was left on the ground, crewman Agg Gardner was pulled 80 feet by a line and broke his leg, and their Parliamentary guest — Malmesbury MP Walter Powell — rose alone into the dusk and was never seen again.

Wreckage of what was presumed to be the balloon, though sans Member of Parliament, would be discovered on the slopes of Sierra del Piedroza in the mountains of Spain [20 January 1882].

Salmet — French aviator **Henri Salmet** was sponsored by the Daily Mail to give air displays around Britain and became the principal pilot at the Louis Bleriot Flying School in Hendon. His popular flight demonstrations included an example of how not to do it when on landing he was blinded by the sun and ran into a tree at Tuckton, between Bournemouth and Christchurch [1913]. The Bleriot monoplane was mangled but Salmet stepped from the wreckage with only a cut to show for it, and his passenger Hatton Turner was unhurt.

One of Salmet's return visits was to Meyrick Park where he delivered Father Christmas, whose time in town just happened to coincide with the absence from his office of department store owner Cyril Beale.

Salter — the world's first female Tornado pilot **Flight-Lieutenant Jo Salter** [born 1968] from Bournemouth qualified as a combat pilot and joined 617 "Dambusters" Squadron at RAF Lossiemouth, Scotland [1995]. "I never feel fear," she was quoted as saying at the press briefing that made her front-page national news. "The Air Force is an armed force and you have to expect to go into combat."

Unmarried, she said she was "just one of the boys", but left future options open: "I would like to have children one day and in the Air Force you can have maternity leave. But I would hate to give up my career."

Her training had cost the RAF £3 million, the same as her male counterparts, and she received a permanent commission which will last until 2007.

Jo Salter would be taken to task for her "never feel fear" remark, and find an able defender in sometime Lieutenant-Commander John Kilbracken RNVR, writing as Lord Kilbracken: "It was far from being my experience, during five wartime years, flying mostly Swordfish biplanes, that all pilots have 'a healthy fear for their aircraft'.

"Fear may come when the flak starts flying or the elastic breaks (our euphemism for the engine failing), but no one should be flying who ever feels afraid when at the controls of a magnificent, well-maintained flying machine in peacetime, except in a dire emergency."

Sandbanks Royal Naval Air Station — known to Poole people as HMS *Tadpole*, because it functioned as the Royal Navy Seaplane School and handled beginners with float-planes that were dwarfed by the flying-boats of British Overseas Airways Corporation and Coastal Command that were the regular users of Poole Harbour. Established for training Fleet Air Arm pilots as a satellite station to HMS *Daedalus* shore-base at Lee-on-Solent [15 May 1940]. Situated on the north-west side of the peninsula where it requisitioned the Royal Motor Yacht Club (Ordnance Survey map reference SZ 044 877).

Withdrew to Lee-on-Solent as the offensive war became busier, with Poole Harbour filling with flying-boats and invasion craft [15 October 1943].

Sandes — Spitfire flyer **Pilot Officer L.D. Sandes** of RAF Warmwell was awarded the Distinguished Flying Cross. He would be killed, aged twenty-eight [26 March 1941], and is buried in the RAF plot at Warmwell cemetery.

Saville — "Missing in Action" **Flight-Lieutenant John Saville** of 439 (Royal Canadian Air Force) Squadron, flying a rocket-firing Typhoon from RAF Hurn [5 June 1944], epitomised the skill, courage and sacrifice of the aerial contribution that caused the D-Day landings to be relatively unopposed. For a Guernsey diver, Mick Peters, would find the remains of lost Typhoon MN210 [1982]. It lies near Moulinet Reef in Havelet Bay, where it had been downed by German flak as the Typhoons destroyed German radar apparatus at Fort George, in the vital "blinding" of the enemy's early-warning system before the invasion armada embarked.

It had been his third attack on Fort George. Not only had he taken part in a raid carried out by 439 Squadron and 440 Squadron two days earlier [3 June 1944], but Johnny Saville had also made a sortie to the same target earlier on D-Day minus 1. In the 1980s, divers were authorized to remove all small surface items that might attract looters — such as a silk parachute which was in mint condition — but the Ministry of Defence discouraged further investigation of the site because of the likelihood that human remains were present.

Schneider International Seaplane Race — known as the Schneider Trophy, donated by French munitions heir Jacques Schneider, resumed off Dorset after the Great War with its third race being held in Poole Bay [10 September 1919]. The contest was between seaplanes, which at this time were biplanes with floats, and it started from Bournemouth Pier with an anti-clockwise circuit of 20 nautical miles via turning points off Durlston Head and Hengistbury Head.

The Royal Navy battleships HMS *Barham* and HMS *Malaya*, both of 31,100-tons and mounting eight 15-inch guns, anchored inside the triangle.

Elite flyers arrived from all over Britain and much of war-torn Europe. What followed was a fiasco.

Lunch and what went with it, aboard the yacht *Ombra*, clouded the judgment of the organising officials from the Royal Aero Club. They overlooked the restricted and deteriorating visibility and proceeded to start the race in a thick "sea-fret" as one of the Bournemouth residents called it. Fog caused chaos and the race was called off, a new time set, and then brought forward by an hour. This effectively disqualified the French team who were using the extra time to repair their floats.

The revised time still had the flyers going off into both fog and dusk. As the light failed the leading aeroplane, a Savoia flying-boat flown by Guido Jannello, made its turns at a reserve buoy moored in Studland Bay, instead of continuing down to the south-eastern corner of the Purbeck coast. This gave the Italian team an astonishing lead, though as it was virtually dark no one had a clear idea of where anyone had flown.

The Royal Aero Club compounded the problem by first declaring the race void, then accepting an Italian appeal and awarding Jannello the £1,000 prize, and having this decision revoked by the Federation Aeronautique Internationale.

An incidental hiccup was the sinking of Supermarine Sea Lion G-EALP, which had been flown by Commander Basil Hobbs, off Bournemouth Pier. It was later lifted, taken to pieces on the beach, and sent to London where it was reassembled and put on display in the Science Museum.

School of Air Traffic Control — established at Hurn Aerodrome to teach the new art of air traffic management [1949-62]. Radar, blind-landing, and queue stacking techniques revolutionised the possibilities for the mass movement of people and planes, with operations around the clock. Britain's first generation of experts learnt their trade in Bournemouth.

SD — Squadron code on the Mark IIa Spitfires of 501 (City of Bristol) Squadron, flying from RAF Ibsley, between Ringwood and Fordingbridge, and regular visitors to the Dorset sky [1941-1942]. They provided evocative wartime footage for the film *The First of the Few*, which was filmed at Ibsley and over the Isle of Wight.

Sea crashes — virtually countless off the Dorset coast during World War Two; in my books on the conflict I have detailed well over a hundred losses and the total must be at least double. Upwards of three-quarters belonged to the Luftwaffe.

In this present book the "Crashes" entry lists a representative quantity from both sides. Post-war losses have been in the testing and training of military aircraft.

An RAF Hunter ditched in the sea off Dorset [15 July 1968] . The pilot was rescued.

An RAF Phantom was lost off the Dorset coast with its two crew killed [13 May 1970] .

Sea Venom — jet fighter, produced for the Fleet Air Arm by the de Havilland factory at Somerford, Christchurch [1950s].

Sea Vixen — jet fighter, produced for the Royal Navy and its aircraft-carriers by the de Havilland factory at Somerford, through the late 1950s and up to the plant's closure and removal to Chester [1962].

Sea Vixen XJ580, the last to fly for the Royal Navy [1982] went to Flight Refuelling Limited at Hurn, and was then purchased by the Sea Vixen Society [1984] for return to Somerford as a "tribute to the aviation history of Christchurch, 1932-62".

7C — squadron code of 296 Squadron, flying Albemarle troop-carriers from RAF Hurn [1943].

Shaftesbury crashes — rising to fly over Dorset's hilltop town, during the Baffle of Britain, Spitfire L1702 of 238 Squadron collided with Hurricane N2474 [30 September 1940].

The Heinkel He. lll flown by Hauptmann Langar, officer commanding the elite Kampfgruppe 100, flew into a hillside near Shaftesbury whilst trying to escape from an interception directed by Sopley radar station [23 May 1942]. The attacking Beaufighter of 604 Squadron was flown by Squadron Leader John "Cat's Eyes" Cunningham from RAF Middle Wallop. Langar had lost his bearings in dense cloud and rain. No shot had been fired.

Shepperd — Spitfire flyer Sergeant Pilot Edmund Eric Shepperd [1917-40] of 152 Squadron from RAF Warmwell claimed four kills during the Battle of Britain: a Messerschmitt Bf.109 [25 July 1940]; a Junkers Ju.88 [12 August 1940]; a Junkers Ju.87 [18 August 1940]; and a second Ju.88 [7 October 1940]. He was killed when his fighter unaccountably plunged into the ground at Tadnoll Mill, north of Chaldon Herring [18 October 1940].

He is buried at Binstead, where he was born, in the Isle of Wight.

Sherborne crash — at Burdon's Nurseries, Oborne Road, of a Hurricane belonging to 87 Squadron from RAF Bibury, Gloucestershire, which was one of the defending aircraft on the afternoon when the town was devastated by Luftwaffe bombs [16.40 hours, 30 September 1940]. Sergeant Pilot Herbert Walton baled out and was taken to the Yeatman Hospital, Sherborne, with minor injuries.

Shillingstone crash — at "Nutmead" [7 October 1940], but this has been found to be an error for Netmead, Child Okeford, and is described under the entry for that parish.

Short — **Spitfire flyer Sergeant Pilot Jimmy Short** of 152 Squadron from RAF Warmwell parachuted into captivity when his fighter was shot down by Messerschmitt Bf.109s as he escorted Hampden bombers that were attacking the French port of Brest [24 July 1941].

Silver City Airways — transferred their fleet of Bristol 170 Wayfarers, better known as the Bristol Freighter, from Southampton to Bournemouth (Hum) Airport [1959]. Ran a constant summertime car-ferry shuttle service from Hum to the Channel Islands.

622 Gliding School — based at Christchurch Aerodrome until its move to Old Sarum, Wiltshire [1963], and from there to Upavon.

Smith — novelist **Frederick Escreet Smith** author of *633 Squadron* and thirty other successful novels lives in Hathaway Road, Southbourne, Bournemouth.

Smith — Typhoon flyer Pilot Officer Graham Smith of 263 Squadron was killed when he failed to pull out of a low roll whilst taking part in the official welcome for the 474th Fighter Group of the United States Army Air Force on their arrival at RAF Warmwell [12 March 1944].

Solway — one of the two Sunderland flying-boat hulks abandoned in Poole Harbour when British Overseas Airways Corporation departed for Southampton Water [1948]. *City of Liverpool* was the other.

Solway was the outer of the two fuselages stranded at Lower Hamworthy, where they were finally beached like stranded whales [1958-59].

She had been built as Short's S.1307 and converted to a Mark 2 Solent, call-sign G-AHIU.

Sopley — **RAF Sopley** radar station [1940-74] began operations with the deployment of a mobile Type 15 ground-to-air antenna, in a field four miles north of Christchurch, on the estate of Lord Manners between the River Avon and the New Forest [25 December 1940]. The radar unit had been developed by the Telecommunications Research Establishment at Worth Matravers and built at Somerford, Christchurch, by the Air Defence Experimental Establishment.

Experiments began with aerial interceptions, through combat guidance to 604 Squadron at RAF Middle Wallop, and the two stations celebrated their first radar-controlled kill three months later [4 March 1941].

What became Southern Radar continued to operate from its underground bunker through the height of the Cold War. "Through freedom to the stars" and "Guard the Flight" declared its mottos. Above-ground buildings at the station became a camp for refugees from the Vietnam war [1978].

Southbourne Aerodrome — laid out as a 3,140-yard racecourse between Belle Vue Road and Church Road in Bournemouth's eastern suburb, created for a major pioneering aviation meeting [1910], and now remembered on a plaque [1978] in the grounds of St Peter's School in St Catherine's Road (Ordnance Survey map reference SZ 147 915): "This stone commemorates the Hon. CHARLES STEWART ROLLS who was killed in a flying accident near this spot on the 12th July 1910, the first Briton to die in powered flight."

Other early aviators who attended the meeting, and survived a number of lesser mishaps, included Edmond Audemars, in *Demoiselle* (crashed) and *Infuriated Grasshopper*; George A. Barnes in *Humber*; Louis Bleriot, as guest visitor; "Colonel" Samuel Franklin Cody in *Cody's Cathedral*; Claude Grahame-White, taking up passengers in his *Autobus*; Captain Bertram Dickson in a Farman biplane; and Leon Morane, winning the sea-flight race; plus a Wright Brothers' *Flyer* from the new production line at Shorts' Shellbeach factory in the Isle of Sheppey, Kent.

Special Duties Flight — under the control of the Air Ministry and put at the disposal of the Christchurch-based Air Defence and Research Development Establishment at Worth Matravers. Arrived at Christchurch Aerodrome, from St Athan, Glamorgan [8 May 1940]. It then comprised six Ansons, four Blenheims, two Harrows, two Fairey Battles, and three "Special Aircraft". These were adapted versions of the Hurricane and Anson and a High Altitude Machine.

Among their first tasks, using three Ansons, was to attempt to track the course of a German "beam", a radio directional signal for the navigation of bombers [21 June 1940].

Blenheim P4832, flown by Flight-Lieutenant Douglas L. Rayment, would be lost over the English Channel, 33 miles south of St Alban's Head, when he told his gunner, Sergeant R. Sadler, to engage a mystery object which they spotted floating on the sea: "There you are, have a go. You can't miss!" Two bursts of machine-gun fire were followed by the aircraft's radio going dead [17 July 1941].

The flight moved from Christchurch to take control of the brand new RAF Hurn [1 August 1941]. After having completed the move it was renamed, as the Research Section of recently formed Telecommunications Flying Unit [10 November 1941].

Squadrons operating from Dorset in World War Two:

19 Squadron — briefly flew Mark Vb Spitfires from RAF Warmwell [1-14 June 1942]. Motto: "Possunt quia posse videntur" - "They can because they think they can". Squadron code: "QV".

41 Squadron — briefly flew Mark XIV Spitfires from RAF Warmwell [7-18 March 1945]. Motto: "Seek and destroy". Squadron code: "PN".

66 Squadron — flew Spitfires from RAF Hurn on escort duties, to protect American Flying Fortress bombers as they crossed the English Channel on daylight raids [10-14 July 1943]. Motto: "Cavete praemonui" - "Beware, I have given warning". Squadron code "RB".

118 Squadron — briefly flew Mark I and IIa Spitfires from RAF Warmwell [9-18 April 1941]. Motto: "Occido redeoque" - "I kill and return". Squadron code: "NK".

125 (Newfoundland) Squadron — flew Mark XVII Mosquito night-fighters from RAF Hurn [25 March - 31 July 1944]. They were controlled by Starlight, as Sopley radar was codenamed, and carried out defensive interceptions over central southern England during the D-Day period. Motto: "Nunquam domandi" - "Never to be tamed". Squadron code: "VA".

130 Squadron — briefly flew Spitfires from RAF Warmwell, with a mix of Mark IIa, Va, and Vb machines [30 November - 5 December 1941]. Motto: "Strong to serve". Squadron code: "AP".

131 (County of Kent) Squadron — flew Spitfires from RAF Hurn on escort duties, to protect American Flying Fortresses as they crossed the English Channel on daylight raids [10-14 July 1943]. Motto: "Invicta" - "Unconquered". Squadron code: "NX".

152 (Hyderabad) Squadron — posted from RAF Acklington, Northumberland, flying into RAF Warmwell with Mark I Spitfires as the Battle of Britain gained momentum [12 July 1940]. Later equipped with Mark II Spitfires [14 March 1941] as losses were replaced. They were transferred to the newly opened RAF Portreath, Cornwall [9 April 1941]. Motto: "Faithful Ally". Squadron Code: "UM".

164 (Argentine-British) Squadron — flew Mark IV Hurricanes from RAF Warmwell [20 June - 6 August 1943]. Returned with Mark Ib Typhoons to RAF Hurn, shortly after D-Day [20 June - 17 July 1944]. Motto: "Firmes Volamos" - "Firmly we fly". Squadron code: "FJ".

170 (Army Co-Operational) Squadron — flew Mustangs from RAF Hurn, in forward reconnaissance and army-support rôles [1942]. Squadron code: "BN".

174 (Mauritius) Squadron — flew Mark IIb Hurricanes from RAF Warmwell [1-21 September 1942]. Motto: "Attack". Squadron code: "XP".

175 Squadron — formed at RAF Warmwell and equipped with Mark IIb Hurricanes [3 March 1942]. They departed in the autumn to RAF Harrowbeer, Devon [10 October 1942], and returned briefly with Mark Ib Typhoons [21 November - 4 December 1944]. Motto: "Stop at nothing". Squadron code: "HH".

181 Squadron — flew rocket-firing Mark Ib Typhoons from RAF Hurn through the D-Day period [1 April - 20 June 1944]. Came back to Dorset in the winter, to RAF Warmwell [12 January - 3 February 1945]. Motto: "Irriumus vastatum" - "We rush in and destroy". Squadron code: "EL".

182 Squadron — flew rocket-firing Mark Ib Typhoons from RAF Hurn through the D-Day period [1 April - 20 June 1944]. Came back to Dorset in the winter, to RAF Warmwell [3-21 February 1945]. Motto: "Fearless I direct my flight". Squadron code: "XM".

183 (Gold Coast) Squadron — flew rocket-firing Mark Ib Typhoons from RAF Hurn during the Battle of Normandy [1-14 July 1944]. Motto: "Versatility". Squadron code: "HF".

184 Squadron — flew Mark Ib Typhoons from RAF Warmwell [4 - 18 December 1944] and returned at the end of the war [7-28 May 1945].

193 (Fellowship of Bellows) Squadron — flew rocket-firing Mark Ib Typhoons from RAF Hurn during the Battle of Normany [3-14 July 1944]. Motto: "Aera et terrain imperare" - "To govern the air and the earth". Squadron code: "DP".

197 Squadron — flew Mark Ib Typhoons from RAF Hurn during the Battle of Normandy [3-20 July 1944]. Motto: "Findimus caelum" - "We cleave the sky". Squadron code: "OV".

198 Squadron — flew rocket-firing Mark Ib Typhoons from RAF Hurn shortly after D-Day [22 June - 1 July 1944]. Motto: "Igni renatus" - "Born again in fire". Squadron code: "TP".

210 Squadron — flew Catalina flying-boats of Coastal Command on long-range anti-submarine patrols over the Atlantic, from RAF Hamworthy [May - December 1943]. Motto: "Yn y nwyfre yn hedfan" - "Hovering in the heavens". Squadron code: "DA".

217 Squadron — flew Avro Ansons on coastal patrols, from RAF Warmwell [1939-40]. Motto: "Woe to the unwary". Squadron code: "MW".

234 (Madras Presidency) Squadron — flew into RAF Warmwell with Mark I Spitfires [24 February 1941].

Changed to Mark II Spitfires, improvised with an unjettisonable fuel drop-tank added to the centre of the port wing, to extend their flying range for escort duties on offensive operations against the Brest peninsula [2 July 1941]. These dismayed the pilots who were appalled at the compromising of the fighter's legendary manoeuvrability. Towards the end of the year they were transferred to RAF Ibsley, Hampshire [5 November 1941], where they would be re-equipped with Mark Vb Spitfires. From this aerodrome, between Ringwood and Fordingbridge, they continued to be regular visitors to Dorset skies.

They returned to RAF Warmwell [23 March 1942], but only for a fortnight, before moving on to Cornwall.

Motto: "Ignem mortemque despuimu" - "We spit fire and death". Squadron code "AZ".

241 Squadron — flew Short and Wright float-planes from Portland Royal Naval Air Station and operated DH6 patrol aircraft from Chickerell Aerodrome, on being formed at the close of the Great War [August - December 1918]. Motto "Find and forewarn".

245 (Northern Rhodesia) Squadron — briefly flew Mark Ib Typhoons from RAF Warmwell [19 December 1944 - 6 January 1945]. Squadron code not known.

247 (China-British) Squadron — briefly flew rocket-firing Mark Ib Typhoons from RAF Hurn through the D-Day period [24 April - 20 June 1944]. Came back to Dorset in the winter, to RAF Warmwell [21 February - 7 March 1945]. Motto: "Rise from the east". Squadron code: "ZY".

253 (Hyderabad State) Squadron — operated DH6 patrol aircraft on coastal anti-submarine flights from Chickerell Aerodrome, at its formation towards the close of the Great War [June - August 1918]. Motto: "Come one, come all".

257 (Burma) Squadron — flew Mark Ib Typhoons from RAF Warmwell [8 January - 12 August 1943] and then returned a month later [17 September 1943 - 20 January 1944]. They were briefly posted to RAF Hurn during the Battle of Normandy [2-8 July 1944]. Motto: "Thay myay gyee shin shwe hti" - "Death or glory". Squadron code: "FM".

263 Squadron — flew Whirlwinds from RAF Warmwell [19-23 December 1941] and returned the following autumn [13 September 1942 - 20 February 1943]. After a short break they were back again [15 March - 19 June 1943] and then re-equipped with Mark Ib Typhoons [12 July - 5 December 1943]. They came back to Warmwell in the spring [6-19 March 1944]. During the Battle of Normandy they were briefly stationed at RAF Hurn [10-23 July 1944]. Motto: "Ex ungue leonem " - "From his claws one knows the lion". Squadron code: "HE".

266 (Rhodesia) Squadron — flew Mark Ib Typhoons from RAF Warmwell [21 September 1942 - 8 January 1943]. Briefly stationed at RAF Hurn during the Battle of Normandy [13-20 July 1944]. Motto: "Hlabezezulu" - "The stabber of the sky". Squadron code: "ZH".

277 Squadron — operated three Walrus amphibians and six Air-Sea Rescue Spitfires from RAF Warmwell [1943-44] and RAF Hurn [18-29 August 1944]. They then returned to Warmwell Aerodrome. Motto: "Quaerendo servamus" — "We save by seeking". Squadron code: "BA".

295 Squadron — flew Halifax tug-planes towing Horsa gliders, from RAF Hurn [1943-44], temporarily departing to take part in airborne landings during the invasion of Sicily [9 July 1943]. Left for RAF Harwell [14 March 1944] Motto: "In caelo auxilium" - "Aid from the skies". Squadron code: "EE".

296 (Army Co-Operational) Squadron — flew Whitleys from RAF Hurn, making paratroop drops for the 1st Airborne Division [1942]. Re-equipped with Albemarle troop-carriers and left to take part in the invasion of Sicily [9 July 1943]. Left for RAF Harwell [14 March 1944] Motto: "Prepared for all things". Squadron code: "7C".

297 (Army Co-Operation) Squadron — flew Whitleys from RAF Hurn [1942] on Special Duties across the Channel, dropping agents for the Special Operations Executive and supplies for resistance groups. Squadron code: "LS".

298 Squadron — flew Halifax tug-planes, towing gliders, from RAF Tarrant Rushton [1943 - 44]. Motto: "Silent we strike". Squadron code: "8A".

302 (Poznanski) Squadron — flew Hurricane IIb fighters from RAF Warmwell [5 September - 11 October 1941] and returned briefly, re-equipped with the Mark Vb Spitfire [27 April - 1 May 1942]. They were a Polish squadron. Squadron code: "WX".

312 Squadron — a Czech unit, briefly flew Mark Vb and Vc Spitfires from RAF Warmwell [20-24 April 1942; 19-31 May 1942] and then made a longer return visit [20 February - 14 March 1943]. Motto: "Non multi sed multa" - "Not many men but many deeds". Squadron code: "DU".

401 (Royal Canadian Air Force / Ram) Squadron — briefly flew Mark IXb Spitfires from RAF Warmwell [24 October - 4 November 1944]. Motto: "Mors cellerima hostibus" - "Very swift death to the enemy". Squadron code: "YO".

402 (Royal Canadian Air Force / Winnipeg Bear) Squadron — flew Mark IIb Hurricanes from RAF Warmwell, on ground-attack offensive sweeps over Normandy and Brittany [6 November 1941 - 4 March 1942]. These were the "Hurri-bomber" variant of the Hawker Hurricane.

The squadron returned to Warmwell with Mark XIVe Spitfires [14 January - 2 February 1945]. Squadron code: "AE".

403 (Royal Canadian Air Force) Squadron — briefly flew Mark XVI Spitfires from RAF Warmwell [4-14 January 1945]. Motto: "Stalk and strike". Squadron code: "KH".

411 (Royal Canadian Air Force) Squadron — briefly flew Mark IXe Spitfires from RAF Warmwell [15-23 October 1944]. Motto: "Inimicus inimico" - "Hostile to an enemy". Squadron code "DB".

412 (Royal Canadian Air Force) Squadron — briefly flew Mark Vb Spitfires from RAF Hurn [1-6 March 1943]. Motto: "Promptus advindtictum" - "Swift to avenge". Squadron code: "VZ".

418 (City of Edmonton) Squadron — briefly flew Mark II Mosquito night-fighters from RAF Hurn, during the Battle of Normandy [14-29 July 1944]. Motto: "Piyautailili" - "Defend even unto death". Squadron code: "TH".

438 (Royal Canadian Air Force) Squadron — flew Mark IV Hurricanes from RAF Hurn [18 March - 3 April 1944] and returned re-equipped with rocket-firing Mark Ib Typhoons for the D-Day period [19 April - 27 June 1944]. Came back to Dorset the following spring, to RAF Warmwell [19 March - 3 April 1945]. Motto: "Going down". Squadron code: "F3".

439 (Royal Canadian Air Force) Squadron — flew Mark IV Hur-

ricanes from RAF Hurn [18 March - 2 April 1944] and returned for
another short period [19 April - 11 May 1944]. They were then re-
equipped with rocket-firing Mark Ib Typhoons and were stationed at
Hurn through the D-Day period [20 May - 27 June 1944]. Came back to
Dorset, to RAF Warmwell, towards the end of the war [3-22 April 1945].
Motto: "Fangs of death". Squadron code: "5V".

440 (Royal Canadian Air Force) Squadron — flew Mark IV Hurricanes from RAF Hum [18 March - 3 April 1944] and returned re-
equipped with Mark Ib Typhoons for the D-Day period [20 April - 28
June 1944]. Came back to Dorset, to RAF Warmwell, for the final fortnight of the war [23 April - 8 May 1945]. Motto: "Ka Ganawaitah
Saguenay" - "He who guards the Saguenay". Squadron code: "I8".

443 (Royal Canadian Air Force / Hornet) Squadron — briefly flew
Mark IXb Spitfires from RAF Warmwell [18 December 1944 - 3 January
1945]. Motto: "Our sting is death". Squadron code: "2I".

461 (Royal Australian Air Force) Squadron — flew Sunderland
flying-boats from RAF Hamworthy [31 August 1942 - 21 April 1943].
Carried out anti-submarine duties for Coastal Command in the English
Channel and South-Western Approaches. Motto: "They shall not pass
unseen". Squadron code: "UT".

504 (County of Nottingham) Squadron — flew Spitfires from RAF
Hurn on escort duties, to protect American Flying Fortress bombers as
they crossed the English Channel on daylight raids [10-14 July 1943].
Motto: "Vindicat in ventis" - "It avenges the wind". Squadron code:
"TM".

570 Squadron — flew Albemarle troop and glider transports from
RAF Hum. Left for Brize Norton [14 March 1944]. Motto: "Impetum
deducimus" - "We launch the spearhead". Squadron code "E7".

601 (County of London) Squadron — its Hurricanes were visitors
to RAF Warmwell, to escort war Premier Winston Churchill to Paris, for
secret talks on the collapse of France after the German invasion [31 May
1940]. Squadron code: "UF".

604 (County of Middlesex) Squadron — flew Mark XIII
Mosquitoes from RAF Hum, through the D-Day period [3 May - 13 July
1944]. Motto: "Si vis pacem, para bellum" - "If you want peace, prepare
for war". Squadron code: "RAK".

609 (West Riding) Squadron — flew Mark I Spitfires from RAF Warmwell, throughout the Battle of Britain. Initially they were day visitors to the station, from Middle Wallop, Hampshire, to which they returned each night [16 July - 2 October 1940]. They then were based full-time at Warmwell [until 24 February 1941]. Motto: "Tally Ho!". Squadron Code "PR".

633 Squadron — fictional Royal Air Force unit created by Bournemouth author Frederick Escreet Smith, based around the real-life precision bombing raids carried out by Mosquitoes during the final year of the war in Europe.

644 Squadron — flew Halifax tug-planes, towing gliders, from RAF Tarrant Rushton [1943-44]. Motto: "Dentes draconis serimus" - "We saw the dragon's teeth". Squadron code: "9U".

737 Royal Naval Air Squadron — reformed with Westland Whirlwind helicopters for airborne anti-submarine training at Portland Royal Naval Air Station [24 April 1959].

765 Fleet Air Arm Squadron — operated Walrus amphibians and Seafox float-planes, later Vought Kingfisher float-planes, from Royal Naval Air Station Sandbanks [June 1941 - 15 October 1943].

772 Fleet Air Arm Squadron — flew Swordfish biplanes as a Fleet Requirements Unit in Portland Harbour [September 1939], attached to the Anti-Submarine School, until removal to Dunoon and Campbelltown following the Luftwaffe's occupation of airfields on the Cherbourg peninsula [July 1940].

793 Fleet Air Arm Squadron — trained at Chickerell Aerodrome [1939-40].

815 Royal Naval Air Squadron — flew Lynx helicopters from Portland Royal Naval Air Station in anti-submarine training flights [1975-88].

829 Royal Naval Air Squadron — flew Lynx helicopters from Portland Royal Naval Air Station in anti-submarine training flights [1975-90].

Stainforth — Weymouth College old boy **Wing Commander George Stainforth** [killed October 1942] rose to fame in 1931 when he took the world airspeed record in Schneider trophy flights.

He pushed his Supermarine S-6B round the Spithead course at an average speed of 340 miles per hour and raised the world's absolute speed record to 379.05 mph. Other records included flying upside down for a duration of eleven minutes seven seconds and the title of RAF revolver champion.

Finally, as Wing Commander in the Middle East, he was the oldest fighter pilot serving in that theatre. He was shot down in night fighting, his particular forte.

Stalbridge crash — of Lysander L6860 belonging to 41 Operational Training Unit of the Royal Air Force [7 October 1941].

Staples — Spitfire flyer **Pilot Officer Michael Staples** of 609 Squadron from RAF Warmwell was shot down in one of the dog-fights over the Blackmore Vale following the bombing of the Westland Aircraft factory at Yeovil [7 October 1940]. He was seriously injured in the leg and baled out at 21,000 feet, as the fighter began its plunge into riverside meadows at Child Okeford. Staples recovered in Blandford Cottage Hospital.

Starfish — codename of the Major Strategic Night Decoy at the west end of Brownsea Island in Poole Harbour. It successfully drew bombs intended for RAF Hamworthy [25 May 1942] and saved Poole and Bournemouth from a total of 1,000 tons of high explosive.

Starlight — codename for RAF Sopley, north of Christchurch, for its direction of night-fighters to intercept German aircraft [1942-44].

Station 416 — Advance Landing Group Christchurch, converted into a base for P-47 Thunderbolt fighter-bombers [7 March - 11 July 1944] of the 9th United States Army Air Force by laying temporary wire-mesh runways across the grass at Christchurch Aerodrome, Somerford.

Station 454 — RAF Warmwell during its secondment to the 474th Fighter Group of the United States Army Air Force [12 March -15 August 1944], flying Lockheed P-38 Lightnings.

Strange — pioneer aviator **Lieutenant-Colonel Louis Arbon Strange** [1891-1966] farmed at Worth Matravers and is buried in the village churchyard. He served in the Great War, winning the Distinguished Service Order, Distinguished Flying Cross and Military Cross.

Between the wars he was a director of Spartan Aircraft until, as Spartan Airlines Limited, it merged with Hillman's Airways and United Airways [1935]. Establishing the Isle of Purbeck Light Aeroplane Club [1926] was followed by London-Berlin non-stop flights in his Simmonds Spartan with two up [24 October 1928]. The return flight was also non-stop and two up [27 October 1928]. These exploits are documented in his memoirs, *Recollections of an Airman* [1933]. He returned to the sky for combat in the Second World War and added a bar to his DFC.

The place at Worth where he used to land became known as Aerodrome Field — indeed he called it "Swanage Aerodrome" — and was subsequently the village football pitch.

Stratton crash — what appears to have been a Junkers Ju.87 "Stuka" or a Messerschmitt Bf.110 fighter-bomber crashed behind Grimstone viaduct, in Stratton parish, as the RAF ripped through the Luftwaffe's Adlertag (Eagle Day) attack [13 August 1940].

Studland crashes — on the beach, then a minefield, by Flying Officer Alexander Rothwell Edge's Spitfire, of 609 Squadron from RAF Warmwell [18 July 1940]. Though covered by sea it would be salvaged and fly again. Edge, who was unhurt, was picked up by the Royal Navy.

Later in the Battle of Britain, a returning Heinkel He.111 bomber that had taken part in devastating the Bristol Aeroplane Company's works at Filton [25 September 1940], crash-landed at Westfield Farm, Studland. Wine waiter Theo Janku took the crew prisoner with an unloaded Home Guard rifle; villagers treated them kindly when it was realised there were casualties. Flight mechanic Josef Attrichter died a few minutes later.

Their bomber (G1+BH) belonged to Kampfgeschwader 55 and the kill was claimed by Hurricanes of 238 Squadron from RAF Middle Wallop.

The Heinkel was relatively undamaged and would be salvaged and reassembled for Cardiff war weapons week.

Sturminster Marshall crashes — Heinkel He.111 (1G+AC), returning to France after bombing Bristol docks, crashed in flames at Sturminster Marshall [12 August 1940]. It belonged to Kampfgeschwader 27 and was being flown by a Gruppenkommander.

During the Cold War an F-111 swing-wing fighter-bomber of the 20th Tactical Wing of the United States Air Force plunged into a hill half a mile from Mapperton, west of Sturminster Marshall [29 April 1980]. The crewmen were Jack Hines of Pennsylvania and Richard Franks of New York. Both were killed, and the impact left a 15-feet crater with wreckage strewn over 500 yards. Cattle panicked in the fields.

It was the second F-111 that had come low over Winterborne Zelston, Bere Regis, and then the hamlet of Almer. The first plane was not involved in the crash and returned safely to its base, Upper Heyford in Oxfordshire. They had been on a routine training flight and were unarmed.

Royal Navy helicopters later landed to help collect wreckage. Because of its sophisticated and secret electronics, Dorset police declared the area a restricted zone.

Mapperton — the farm's placename — caused some confusion for the recovery teams. One helicopter landed at Maperton village near Wincanton (22 miles to the north-west). It dropped into a paddock close to the country mansion of singer Georgie Fame, before realising the mistake.

A kit-built Montgomery-Bensen B8M Autogyro — similar to that flown by Sean Connery as James Bond in the film *You Only Live Twice* — crashed on the north side of the A31 near the Stag Gate entrance to Charborough Park [11 December 1993]. Professional pilot Paul Crook [1936-93], who flew Falcon jets for FR Aviation from Hurn (Bournemouth) Airport, was killed instantly as the "flying motorbike" dropped like a stone. He was on a test flight to decide whether to buy one — there were said to be only fifteen such machines in the country.

Both machine and pilot had been in working order. Crook probably caused the crash, investigators concluded, by his own instinctive fixed-wing reactions. On encountering turbulence, as he climbed to 200-feet, he had moved the control column forward. This would increase the speed of a normal aircraft and therefore create lift. An autogyro handles differently, with its top rotor reducing speed, so the machine stalled and nose-dived.

Sutton Waldron crash — at Vale Farm, of Spitfire X4472 of 609 Squadron from RAF Warmwell, during the dog-fights following the bombing of the Westland Aircraft Company works at Yeovil [16.00 hours, 7 October 1940]. Flight-Lieutenant Frank Howell stayed with his aircraft and made a successful forced-landing. The fighter was repairable.

Swanage Aerodrome — opened with a flying display [16 August 1928] and was located in the parish of Worth Matravers, on The Plain between the village and St Alban's Head. Operated by the Isle of Purbeck Light Aeroplane Club and organised by veteran local flyer Lieutenant-Colonel Louis Strange.

Swanage crashes — of a Messerschmitt Bf.110 in the Battle of Britain, claimed by Flying Officer John Dundas flying a Spitfire of 609 Squadron from RAF Warmwell [11 August 1940].

Brian Sharpe of Tunbridge Wells has informed me of another wartime crash, this time one of ours: "On a Saturday afternoon I recall a Spitfire came low over the bay and town with engine spluttering and crashed through a hedge at Ulwell, close to Godlingston brickworks. I believe the pilot was killed."

There were many more crashes, from both sides, into the sea. Swanage had an RAF Air-Sea Rescue launch that operated in this particularly busy central sector of the English Channel, from Portland Bill in Dorset to St Catherine's Point in the Isle of Wight.

Battle of Britain losses inflicted on the RAF off Swanage included:

Spitfire of 609 Squadron from RAF Warmwell [8 July 1940].

Spitfire R6634 of 609 Squadron shot down by the gunner of a Junkers Ju.88 bomber [18 July 1940].

Spitfire K9880 of 152 Squadron [20 July 1940].

Hurricane P2978 of 238 Squadron [11 August 1940].

Spitfire K9882 of 152 Squadron [26 September 1940].

Swanage RAF Hospital — established towards the end of the Great War for convalescent cases. Captain Clement Perronet Sells of the Royal Army Medical Corps "died on July 4th 1919 at RAF Hospital Swanage, of illness contracted on Active Service, Aged 29 years".

He is buried in Northbrook Road Cemetery. A nearby stone is to Flight-Lieutenant P.L.T. Lewin of the RAF who died on 9 September 1919.

Sydling St Nicholas crashes — of a Messerschmitt Bf.109 shot down at Hundred Acres Field, Spriggs Farm [16.40 hours, 30 September 1940]. It belonged to the 5th Staffel of fighter wing Jagdgeschwader 2 Richthofen. It came from the south and the pilot, Unteroffizier Alois Dollinger, had baled out over Grimstone, near Stratton. The parachute failed to open and he fell to his death. The Black-2 had flown from Octeville, Le Havre, and was escorting the Luftwaffe attack that ended with bombs being jettisoned on Sherborne. This was the longest range of all the Bf.109 crashes of 1940.

A Junkers Ju.88 bomber (9K+SN), heading for the Westland Aircraft factory at Yeovil, was brought down on Tappers Hill, above the hamlet of Up Sydling [16.20 hours, 7 October 1940]. The kill was claimed jointly by Sergeant Pilot Edmund Shepperd of 152 Squadron from RAF Warmwell and Flying Officer Bob Doe in a Hurricane of 238 Squadron from RAF Middle Wallop.

All four members of the German crew baled out successfully and were taken prisoner of war, after being rounded up by shotgun, following which the farm labourers were said to have performed a victory dance around the wreckage. The crewmen were Oberleutnant Sigurd Hey, Leutnant Friedrich Bein, Oberfeldwebel Christian Koenig, and Oberfeldwebel Josef Troll.

The bomber belonged to the 5th Staffel of II Gruppe Kampfgruppe 51.

Symondsbury crash — a Hurricane of 87 Squadron from RAF Exeter successfully crash-landed near the village after attempting to tackle a mass of German aircraft at the peak of the Battle of Britain [15 August 1940].

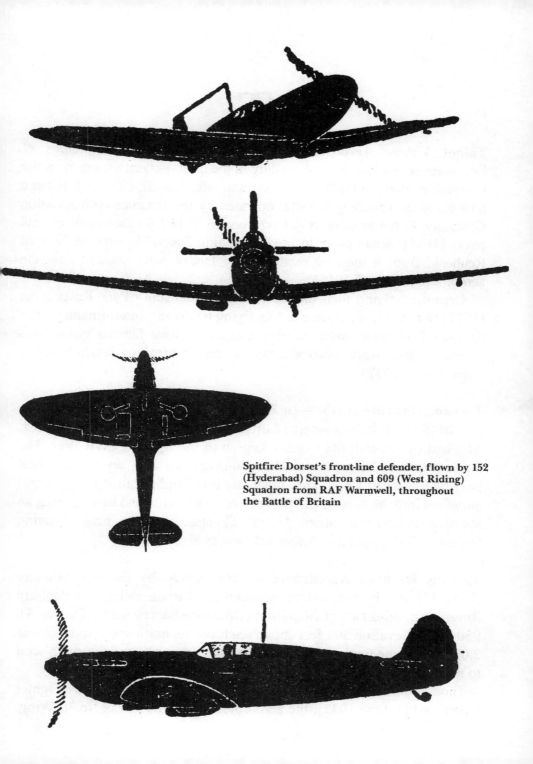

Spitfire: Dorset's front-line defender, flown by 152
(Hyderabad) Squadron and 609 (West Riding)
Squadron from RAF Warmwell, throughout
the Battle of Britain

T

Talbot Village Aerodrome — now covered by the buildings of Bournemouth University and actually in the north-eastern extremity of the Borough of Poole (Ordnance Survey map reference SZ 075 936). It came into being as a training airfield, operated by the Bournemouth Aviation Company, as the Royal Flying Corps issued its call for thousands of new pilots [1915]. Some came to grief, including Second-Lieutenant Edward Rebbeck, from a mayoral estate-agency family, who crashed near the aerodrome [24 April 1916].

Organised flying then moved to the new Ensbury Park Racecourse [1917] but the old field resumed its flying traditions, intermittently, after Ensbury Park went under housing estates. Its final famous visitor was British aviatrix Amy Johnson, after her record-breaking return flight to Cape Town [1932].

Tarrant Gunville crash — at Bussey Stool Farm, of a Messerschmitt Bf.110 (S9+JH) killing veteran Luftwaffe pilot 27-year-old Martin Lutz, who had flown with the Condor Legion in the Spanish Civil War. The fighter-bomber, belonging to Erprobungsgruppe 210, an experimental proving unit from Cherbourg, gradually lost height until it hit trees and ploughed into the ground [27 September 1940]. Lutz had been leading an abortive raid on the Parnall Aircraft Company at Yate, near Chipping Sodbury. Radio operator Anton Schön was also killed.

Tarrant Rushton Aerodrome — constructed by the Air Ministry [1942-43], on chalk downland between the Tarrant valley and Badbury Rings, four miles east of Blandford (Ordnance Survey map reference ST 950 060). Elevation 301 feet above sea level. Its north-south runway was 2,000 yards; the north-west to south-east 1,500 yards; and the south-west to north-east also 1,500 yards.

Though initial control was passed to No.10 Group, RAF Fighter Command [1 June 1943], the aerodrome's main user was No.38 Wing,

Army Co-Operation Command, which was reformed as No.38 Group, Airborne Forces [11 October 1943].

Control of Tarrant Rushton and its 38 Group operators was passed to the Allied Expeditionary Air Force [1 February 1944] in preparation for the invasion of Europe. Its Commander-in-Chief, Air Chief Marshal Sir Trafford Leigh-Mallory visited the station [12 February 1944] and returned with General Dwight D. Eisenhower, the Supreme Commander of Allied Forces in Western Europe [22 April 1944], to see the readiness of the British 6th Air Landing Brigade and its associated 6th Airborne Division.

Exercises, at first at day and then at night, coupled with paratroop drops on Cranborne Chase, were soon to turn to reality. As the preparations for the opening of the Second Front became continuous, geography would give Tarrant Rushton the key position in the unfolding drama, in that it and the overspill field at nearby RAF Hurn lay closer to the selected drop-zones in Normandy than any other major airfields.

Tarrant Rushton would have the distinction of landing the first Allied soldiers to arrive in France on D-Day, with the arrival of Major John Howard and "D" Company of the 2nd Battalion, Oxford and Buckinghamshire Light Infantry. They emerged from their Horsa glider, the first of six in Operation Coup de Main, to seize and to hold the Orne canal bridge [01.30 hours, 6 June 1944] which would henceforth be known as Pegasus Bridge — from the men's flying-horse emblem.

The station then played its part in the two great setbacks of 1944. First the Halifax tug-planes and 96 gliders took the British 1st Airborne Division to Arnhem and its "Bridge too far" [17 September 1944]. This reversal in the tide of war was followed by a second disaster in the bleak midwinter.

Casualties streamed into Dorset, via Tarrant Rushton, as the Germans flung their armour into a final counter-offensive through the snowy forests of the Ardennes [Christmas 1944]. Up to 500 wounded Americans were flown into Tarrant Rushton by C-47 Dakotas in a single night and taken to the 22nd General Hospital of the United States Army, at Blandford Camp.

Sixty Halifax tug-planes and their Hamilcar and Horsa gliders would leave Tarrant Rushton [21 March 1945] for Operation Varsity, in which the British 6th Airborne Division was dropped beyond the Rhine, into Germany [24 March 1945]. Fifty-two of the Tarrant Rushton gliders landed successfully in daytime landings that had to be mounted from an East Anglian airfield within flying range. RAF Woodbridge, Suffolk, was chosen, and with this final airborne offensive of the Second World War Tarrant Rushton ceased to be a front-line air base.

As the war approached its fiftieth anniversaries, though shortly before the collapse of communism, I penned the following tribute to what was being remembered as "the Pegasus Aerodrome" for *Dorset County Magazine*:

Major John Howard had to win the Battle of Pegasus Bridge twice over. The first time he dropped in, after an uneventful flight from Tarrant Rushton Aerodrome in Dorset, with the 1st Platoon of "D" Company of the 2nd Battalion of the Oxfordshire and Buckinghamshire Light Infantry. Minutes into 6 June 1944 they stepped out of their Horsa gliders and opened the Second Front in Normandy. They were the first Allied soldiers to arrive in France on D-Day.

John Howard's second battle at the bridge over the Orne canal was to save the building he had brought to fame, the Pegasus Cafe, when in 1987 the French threatened it with demolition for a road scheme to improve the approaches to Caen for port traffic.

The Dorset field from which his Halifax bomber tug-plane lumbered into the air at 22.56 hours on the night of 5 June 1944 has fared worse. Far from being a focal point for emotional controversy it has languished into obscurity. Though many will probably approve. For it is a modern day example of swords into ploughshares, the great long runway having been transformed into a prairie of wheat and barley. Some hangars survive, partially utilised as barns, but the sky was lifeless and the surroundings silent as I tried to visualise these empty uplands between Badbury Rings and the Tarrant valley as centre-stage for a turning-point in world history.

Only a few square yards cherish the memory. The byway from Tarrant Rushton to Witchampton makes a sudden detour to avoid the airfield which had been constructed across its path. It is a ninety degree bend (Ordnance Survey map reference ST 950 061) beside a hangar, and here is a stone war memorial to the flyers and soldiers they carried to war.

The last time I had been at the spot it had been a little more exciting. A little earlier in the day, in the hot summer of 1959, I had persuaded my father to drive us in his Standard Eight up the narrow lane that ascends the hillside directly above Tarrant Rushton church. It used to be the old road to Witchampton but was cut by the construction of the aerodrome during the war and was physically stopped-up by a gate that should have been locked. That day it was not only open but swung back out of sight; the road suddenly became a runway as it emerged from its hedged confinement into a space that was literally a mile wide.

We drove beside a Valiant, an ex-V bomber converted into a tanker by Flight Refuelling Limited, before turning the little car and seeking out our insignificant hole in the boundary fence. Now however, there is nothing to convey the sheer scale of the operation which was not only to tow the British 6th Airborne Division and unleash it over France but had then to go straight into a repeat the following evening.

Then the two squadrons of Halifax tow-planes from Tarrant Rushton had to be back over Normandy and pulling a convoy of thirty of the heavier, mainly Hamilcar type, gliders of the 6th Air Landing Brigade. These contained the Division's real hardware, with equipment such as Tetrarch tanks, Bren-gun carriers, 25-pounder field guns, scout cars and Bailey bridge pontoons, as well as crates of ammunition and stores.

That success would lead to the euphoria that brought about a defeat. General Dwight D. Eisenhower, the Supreme Commander of Allied Forces in Western Europe, had visited Tarrant Rushton on 22 April 1944. He was totally won over to the concept of airborne landings and would feel D-Day had proved that gliders and paratroops could be used on a far greater scale. The great sequel was Operation Market Garden. "I not only approved Market Garden, I insisted on it," Eisenhower admitted in 1966.

Nearly a hundred Hamilcar gliders, towed by their Halifax tug-planes, lifted off from Tarrant Rushton Aerodrome on the morning of Sunday 17 September 1944 to carry the British 1st Airborne Division to a bridge on the Lower Rhine at Arnhem. In all there were three hundred gliders and paratroop carrying aircraft. Eight thousand men were about to find themselves dropping in on the crack 9th and 10th SS Panzer Divisions under the command of General Field Marshal Walther Model.

That 2,400 of them would, by 26 September, be extricated from the "Bridge too far" was largely due to the efforts of 250 men of 4th Battalion of the Dorsetshire Regiment. They maintained a shuttle service of assault boats, under withering enemy fire, crossing and re-crossing the Lower Rhine to bring weary paratroopers back from the Arnhem bridgehead. As it became light at 6 o'clock on the morning of the 26th the German fire assumed pinpoint accuracy and further rescues were impossible.

Despite the setback the war was moving away from Dorset. On 21 March 1945, the sixty Halifax tug-planes and their Hamilcar and Horsa gliders left Tarrant Rushton for Woodbridge in Suffolk. They were en route to their final landings of the war. This was Operation Varsity which began at 9.45 in the morning of 24 March and lasted three hours. Fifty-two of the Tarrant Rushton gliders landed successfully on the far side of the Rhine and delivered the British 6th Airborne Division on to German soil. They took Hamminkeln and the bridge over the River Issel.

The war closed before the next operation could get into the sky — it would have been Operation Doomsday to capture Oslo airfield — and hereon the Halifax tug-planes were seconded to conventional transport duties.

That might have been the end of the story, bringing the curtain down on a sheep-down that had been converted into one of Europe's major airfields over the winter of 1942, except that it became the main base for Sir Alan Cobham's Flight Refuelling Limited. Their bulk fuel tankers would be requisitioned for the peak moment of "Cold War" tension, in fact in the year when United States presidential adviser Bernard Baruch coined the phrase. Soviet forces in East Germany cut the highway and rail links between West Germany and Berlin on 24 July 1948.

The following day the first of fourteen Lancastrian and Lancaster tankers that would be committed to the operation from Tarrant Rushton was heading towards Gatow. In all they would carry 26,000 tons of fuel in Operation Plainfare—hastily changed from Operation Carter Paterson to avoid the "Removals" theme—and the flights had to be kept up daily until 30 September 1949.

Forty Tarrant Rushton air crew were involved and five of them would be killed when a Flight Refuelling Lancastrian plunged into the Hampshire

Downs near Andover. In vain? Not to the two million people of West Berlin nor perhaps in a wider sense. For the determination to break the Berlin blockade established for both sides, present Allies and Red Army alike, the inviolability of the boundaries that had been drawn across Europe at the end of the war. What they lacked in cartographical neatness would be compensated for in terms of lasting mutual respect.

For Flight Refuelling there came the excitement on 7 August 1949 of enabling a Meteor jet to set an international endurance record — Pat Hornidge kept it in the air for more than twelve hours. In-flight fuelling was on its way to application and acceptability in all the world's major air forces. It would in 1982 enable a Vulcan bomber to fly from Ascension Island a third of the way across the globe to make the first dramatic gesture against the Argentinians holding Port Stanley airfield. Flight Refuelling Limited continues, from a factory on the Stour riverside at Wimborne, but by the early 1970s it no longer needed its own air force or a square mile of Dorset chalkland.

There was just a little token pleasure flying from Tarrant Rushton — in the lightweight one-man descendants of those wartime troop-carrying gliders — and then in 1980 the bulldozers crunched the hardcore and concrete of the runways. From hereon it is just another cornfield that has had a history. It is quite some cornfield. And one hell of a legend.

Tarrant Rushton crashes — remarkably few, in view of its night and day wartime operations, though several gliders were damaged or written-off in mishaps.

As an Advanced Flying School it suffered a wrecked airframe, of a Vampire, following an aborted take-off [June 1953].

Taylor — sole pilot to be killed in an air crash in the history of Flight Refuelling Limited, **Captain Cyril "Pop" Taylor DFC** [1914-48] went off course and flew Lancaster tanker G-AHJW into the Hampshire Downs. Six of his crew were also killed. They were returning empty to their base at Tarrant Rushton, from Berlin.

He and three others are buried in St Mary's churchyard, Andover, beneath this inscription: "Four of the gallant crew of seven who gave their lives for the cause of humanity during the Berlin Airlift operation in an accident at Conholt Park on November 22nd 1948."

Telecommunications Flying Unit — Air Ministry Flight formed at the new Hurn Aerodrome [13 August 1941]. Its Development Section was a regrouping of the former Fighter Establishment from RAF Middle Wallop. Then it absorbed, as its Research Section, the Special Duties Flight which was previously at Christchurch Aerodrome [10 November 1941]. This provided aerial test-beds and laboratories for the pioneering Telecommunications Research Establishment at Worth Matravers and Langton Matravers, on the Purbeck coast.

The Telecommunications Flying Unit, with its collection of some fifty assorted aircraft, left for Defford, near Worcester, when its parent Telecommunications Research Establishment was evacuated to Malvern [25 May 1942].

Telecommunications Research Establishment — moved from Dundee to a new base between Worth Matravers village and Renscombe Farm, with young radio research scientists Alan Hodgkin and Bernard Lovell being among the advance party [26 February 1940]. They would be joined by Dr Robert Cockburn and the establishment would be fully evacuated to Worth by the spring [5 May 1940].

Later in the year it requisitioned Leeson House and Durnford School in the neighbouring village of Langton Matravers. The scientists at Worth and Langton were soon to be deeply involved in the "Battle of the Beams" as the Luftwaffe targeted inland English objectives by an intersection of radio pulses — one of synchronised dots and the other of dashes — transmitted from Kleve, in Germany, near the Dutch border south-east of Arnhem, and from Stolberg near the Danish border.

Dr Cockburn developed a Radio Counter Measure codenamed "Aspirin" which duplicated the continuous morse dashes, transmitted on a frequency of 30 to 31.5 megacycles per second, which disorientated the German pilots by widening their direction beam [September 1940]. As these asynchronous signals were having their desired effect, more sophisticated forms of interference — such as an attempt to "bend" the beam — were not necessary.

They would be the recipients of revelations from priceless prizes beached at West Bay, Bridport, in the form of radio equipment on a pathfinding Heinkel He.111 bomber [6 November 1940].

Scientists at the Royal Aircraft Establishment, Farnborough, reassembled its apparatus which comprised three vertical aerials and an intact X-Gerät radio receiver — also known as Wotan I — which enabled the aircraft, from Kampfgruppe 100, to follow a radio direction beam. What surprised the Air Ministry boffins was that the apparatus was tuned to 2000 cycles per second (approximating to the "C" which is two octaves above standard-pitch middle "C") whereas British jamming countermeasures had assumed a note of 1500 cycles (approximating to the "G" below this upper "C").

The discovery came too late to prevent the Coventry raid but it would ensure that radio countermeasures were perfected in time to save the vital Rolls-Royce aero engine plant at Derby. In moonlit conditions similar to those of the Coventry raid, Derby's bombs fell on Nottingham — and those intended for Nottingham fell into open fields [8 May 1941].

As part of the Battle of the Beams, Dr Robert Cockburn commandeered the BBC's pre-war television transmitter at Alexandra Palace, Muswell Hill, on what turned out to be the very night that the Luftwaffe changed to a frequency of 42.5 megacycles per second. This was jammed by Cockburn in countermeasure "Domino" — in which the German signal was re-radiated back to the attacking aircraft, from Alexandra Palace, at 46.9 megacycles per second.

A second transmitting station, constructed on Beacon Hill, near Salisbury, extended Cockburn's jamming across the whole of southern England.

Other suspicious signals were seeping out of France.

Derek Garrard, an Air Ministry scientist seconded to the Telecommunications Research Establishmnet, drove to St Alban's Head with a VHF radio set and found himself picking up transmissions from the Cherbourg peninsula on the 2.5 metre wavelength [24 February 1941]. The bearings suggested a source in the area of Ayderville, where Flight Officer W.K. Manifould had coincidentally photographed a "Freya" square-mesh turntable aerial only two days before.

Intercepted German radio traffic had credited this device with the sinking, off Portland, of the destroyer HMS *Delight*. As a result of the

Garrard's discovery, Air Marshal Sir Philip Joubert called a meeting with just one item on the agenda: "To discuss the existence of German radar."

The Purbeck scientists also developed British radar innovations, devising the Type 15 ground-to-air antenna which would be built by the Air Defence Experimental Establishment at Somerford, Christchurch, and put into the field at Sopley where it enabled combat guidance, given to 604 Squadron at RAF Middle Wallop, to achieve their first radar-controlled kill [4 March 1941].

The establishment's Special Duty Flight, based at Christchurch Aerodrome, became first user of the newly opened RAF Hurn [1 August 1941].

Wellington T2565, being used by the Telecommunications Research Establishment on a signals probe, was lost over France after engine failure [6 November 1941]. Six of the seven crew were taken prisoner of war but the seventh, Sergeant N.W. MacKenzie, was able to avoid capture and escaped to eventually return to Britain.

Meanwhile, the Special Duty Flight had been renamed the Research Section of the Telecommunications Flying Unit, and continued to be based at RAF Hurn [10 November 1941].

It would now make its most remarkable series of flights, which would enable Air Marshal Sir Arthur Harris, Commander-in-Chief Bomber Command, to mount the massive night raids against German cities. Using an AI (Airborne Interception) Mark VII radar set, installed in a Blenheim bomber but with its centimetric beam tilted towards the ground, scientists found themselves mapping Bournemouth and could distinguish streets and houses from the surrounding landscape of heather and pines.

Professor Philip Dee and his assistant Bernard Lovell presented the results of the initial BN (Blind Navigation) tests to the Secretary of State for Air, Sir Archibald Sinclair, who ordered six more test flights to "determine whether the signals obtained ... could be definitely associated with ground objects [23 December 1941].

Scientists at Worth were to receive their greatest prize courtesy "C" Company of the Second Battalion, the Parachute Regiment, who mounted a commando raid at Bruneval, on the French coast between Le Havre and Fécamp, to capture a German Würzburg radar apparatus [27 February

1942]. This comprised a parabolic aerial, receiver, and cathode-ray tube.

On this side of the Channel, TRE's Telecommunications Flying Unit received one of the first Halifax bombers, V9977, fitted with a perspex cupola in the space which would normally have housed the nose gun-turret [22 March 1942]. Here the Purbeck scientists would install the magnetron section of a Mark VII AI (Airborne Interception) radar, adapted into the first prototype of a version codenamed H2S which was being developed for ground-mapping.

These signals would enable the team to spot Bournemouth, from a distance of six miles at a height of 8,000 feet, and to distinguish it from the outlines and land-forms of the adjoining towns of Poole and Christchurch [17 April 1942]. A repeat performance that night would have proved the system in operational conditions — in the dark and through the clouds — except that the operator failed to find a concealed switch and the radar was not turned on.

Tested by Air Commodore Donald "Pathfinder" Bennett and put into production, at a factory in West Howe, Bournemouth. Codenamed H2S, after Professor Frederick Lindemann had exclaimed: "It stinks that it wasn't thought of before." on being given some excuses. Used operationally by Bomber Command to find Hamburg [30-31 January 1943] and henceforth enabled night-bombing of the correct cities for the rest of the war.

The Telecommunications Research Establishment would be evacuated from Worth Matravers and Langton Matravers to Malvern College, Worcestershire, because of fears that the Germans might attempt their own Bruneval-style raid on the Dorset coast [25 May 1942].

Many ideas and projects from Dorset days would be brought into service later in the war, such as the radar-reflective "Window" which created a smoke-screen effect upon enemy radar sets, when dropped in the form of millions of thin strips of aluminium backed paper. This made its operational debut before a big raid on Hamburg [24-25 July 1943]. That night it reduced losses among the 791 participating bombers from an estimated 48, based on normal casualty rates, to only 12.

TH — squadron code of 418 (RCAF City of Edmonton) Squadron, flying Mosquito night-fighters from RAF Hurn [14-29 July 1944].

Thornford crash — Tiger Moth N6658, belonging to 2 Elementary Flying Training School of the RAF, made a forced-landing [9 November 1945].

Tibbets — atom bomb pilot **Major Paul Tibbets** who took B-29 *Enola Gay* (named for his mother) to Hiroshima, ferried VIPs from RAF Hurn earlier in the Second World War. He took Lieutenant-General Dwight D. Eisenhower, then Commander of Allied Forces North-West Africa, to Gibraltar [3 November 1942] for the conference that would put the finishing touches to the invasion of French North Africa.

Tillard — Fleet Air Arm pilot **Lieutenant-Commander Claude Tillard** [1909-41] was born in Wimborne. A torpedo-bomber on the aircraft carrier HMS *Furious* [1935], he became a training officer, and was re-called by the Royal Navy on the outbreak of war. He was given command of 808 Naval Air Squadron, equipped with Fulmars, in dockyard defence at Wick [July 1940] and then took the squadron to sea, aboard HMS *Ark Royal* [October 1940]. He was credited with five kills but was then shot down himself, into the Mediterranean [3 April 1941]. He is buried in the War Cemetery at Enfidaville, Tunisia.

TK — pundit code of RAF Tarrant Rushton, displayed on large letters on the ground and broadcast at night in Morse code, from a mobile beacon.

TM — squadron code of 504 (County of Nottingham) Squadron, flying Spitfires on bomber escort duties from RAF Hurn [10-14 July 1943].

Tobin — American volunteer **Pilot Officer Eugene Quimby "Red" Tobin** [1917-41], a messenger from the MGM Studios in Hollywood, went to fight in Finland and retreated to l'Armée de l'Air in Paris, escaping from the Fall of France to become a Spitfire pilot with 609 Squadron at RAF Warmwell. During the Battle of Britain he claimed half the kills of a Messerschmitt Bf.110 over Chaldon Herring [25 August 1940] and a Dornier Do.17 bomber [15 September 1940].

Unlucky on leaving Dorset, being shot down on 71 Squadron's first sweep over France, from RAF Church Fenton [7 September 1941]. He is buried in the Eastern Cemetery at Boulogne.

Toller Admiralty Airship Station — situated a mile and a half west of the village of Toller Porcorum, in the wooded hills north-west of Gray's Farm, actually in the parish of Powerstock (Ordnance Survey map reference SY 540 980).

Operated as part of No.9 Group, being a satellite station to Mullion, Cornwall, for patrols against German U-boats between Start Point and Portland Bill [spring 1918 - November 1918]. Closed within a month of the end of the Great War.

TP — squadron code of 198 Squadron, flying rocket-firing Typhoons on cross-Channel missions from RAF Hurn [22 June - 1 July 1944].

Trots — series of water runways, marked out by buoys and car tyres, for flying-boats landing and taking off from Poole Harbour [1939-48].

No.1 Trot was off the lake area of Hamworthy; No.2 Trot was off Lower Hamworthy; No.3 Trot was off Parkstone Bay and Lilliput; No.4 Trot was between Brownsea Island and Sandbanks.

The four runways joined to form a continuous taxiing route up the Main Channel and then into Wareham Channel, to the hards at Poole Flying Boat Base, Hamworthy.

Turner — veteran balloonist **Hatton Turner** [born 1840] retired to Bournemouth and went up for a ride in a Bleriot monoplane with French aviator Henri Salmet [1913]. The flight ended in a hedge, with the machine "somewhat severely damaged", after Salmet misjudged the landing and flew into the blinding sun — out of which the flyer walked away with a cut, and Turner without any injury.

2I — squadron code of 443 Squadron, flying Mark IXb Spitfires from RAF Warmwell [18 December 1944 - 3 January 1945].

Tyneham crashes — on Povington Heath of Messerschmitt Bf.110 (2N+EP), in a forced-landing, with the first German flyers to be taken prisoner in the Battle of Britain [11 July 1940]. They were Oberleutnant Gerhard Kadow, pilot, and Gefreiter Helmut Scholz, gunner, of the 9th Staffel, Zerstörergeschwader 76, from Laval. The kill was claimed by Spitfires of 609 Squadron from RAF Warmwell.

Less fortunate were the crew of another Bf.110, almost certainly Hans Carschel and Unteroffizier Klose in 3U+BD of Zerstörergeschwader 26, who crashed at Egliston, between Tyneham and Kimmeridge [27 September 1940]. Their Geschwader was named Horst Wessel after the Nazi writer of a militant anti-Semitic song which became a national anthem. They had been taking part in an abortive raid on the Parnall Aircraft Company at Yate, near Chipping Sodbury.

Typhoon: at its most deadly in the rocket-firing role, flying cross-Channel missions from RAF Hurn for D-Day preparations and the Battle of Normandy, in the summer of 1944

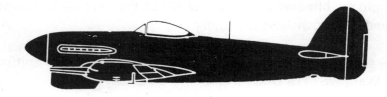

U

UM — code letters of 152 (Hyderabad) Squadron, flying Spitfires from RAF Warmwell [1940-41].

United States Army Air Force — the 31st Fighter Group detachment flew British-made Spitfires, from RAF Warmwell [July 1942].

The 9th USAAF had a number of Dorset bases for the run-up to D-Day and through the Battle of Normandy, with three squadrons each of Republic P-47 Thunderbolts at RAF Christchurch [7 March - 11 July 1944], Lockheed P-38 Lightnings at RAF Warmwell [12 March - 5 August 1944], and Martin B-26 Marauders at RAF Hurn [3 August - 20 August 1944]. The operating formations were the 405th Fighter Bomber Group at Christchurch; the 474th Fighter Group at Warmwell; and the 97th Bombardment Group at Hurn.

Daylight raids over Germany were conducted from further north and east, by the 8th USAAF — comprising the VIIIth Bomber Command, VIIIth Fighter Command and VIIIth Air Service Command. As with British Bomber Command "strays", damaged, disorientated, and out-of-fuel American Flying Fortress and Liberator bombers frequently made emergency landings on Dorset aerodromes.

Upton Admiralty Airship Station — in heathland pines to the west of Poole, operated as a satellite base to Polegate, Sussex, for patrols against German U-boats between Portland Bill and St Catherine's Point, Isle of Wight [1917-18].

Uruguay — an ex-BOAC Mark V Sunderland flying-boat from Poole, converted into a Sandringham-2 for carrying 45 passengers and sold to the Argentine airline Dodero [November 1945].

UT — code letters of 461 (Royal Australian Air Force) Squadron, flying Sunderland flying-boats from RAF Hamworthy [1942-43].

V

VA — squadron code of 125 (Newfoundland) Squadron, flying Mosquito night-fighters from RAF Hurn [25 March - 31 July 1944].

Vampire — jet fighter, produced as trainers by the de Havilland factory at Somerford, Christchurch [1950s].

Varsity landings — the final operation for RAF Tarrant Rushton, carrying the British 6th Airborne Division to Hamminkein and the bridges over the River Issel, on the German side of the Rhine [24 March 1945]. Though 60 Halifax tug-planes and their Hamilcar and Horsa gliders took part from Dorset, of which 52 gliders were to land successfully, they did so by leaving Tarrant Rushton three days earlier and went via a staging-post in East Anglia.

This aerodrome, in range of the German objectives, was RAF Woodbridge, in Suffolk.

Vega — Catalina flying-boat, formerly British Overseas Airways FL, which left Poole Harbour for Trincomalee, Ceylon [17 April 1943] where she was handed over to RAF South-East Asia Command.

Venom — jet fighter, produced by the de Havilland factory at Somerford, Christchurch [1950s].

Ventry — airship-maker **Arthur Frederick Daubeney Olav Eveleigh-de-Moleyns**, seventh **Baron Ventry** [1898-1987], lived at Lindsay Hall, Lindsay Road, Bournemouth. An accident on the ground ended the career of his airship *Bournemouth* at Cardington, Bedfordshire [1951] and with it the post-war fortunes of dirigible flight. The nation had not forgotten that the R101 became a fireball at Beauvais, France, on her maiden voyage to Australia [1930].

Vickers Armstrongs (Aircraft) Limited — one of the premier British aircraft production companies, came to Hurn Aerodrome to flight-test the first V-bomber [June 1951]. The first prototype of the Vickers Valiant flew burning over Bournemouth and crashed at Harrow Farm, Bransgore, on the edge of the New Forest [12 January 1952]. Ultimately it would be premature metal fatigue that would take the Valiants out of RAF service.

Meanwhile, Vickers set up a factory to manufacture their new passenger plane, the Vickers Viscount, with work being shared between Weybridge and Hurn, where the airframes were completed.

Villae de Poole — Spitfire donated by the people of Poole to the newly formed 411 (Royal Canadian Air Force) Squadron [22 June 1941]. It crashed at Chester during a blizzard, killing Sergeant Pilot S.W. Bradshaw [7 December 1941].

Viscount — made by Vickers Armstrongs (Aircraft) Limited, with production being shared between their main works at Weybridge, Surrey, and the factory at Bournemouth (Hurn) Airport [1950s]. Hurn would produce a total of 200.

von Dalwigk — "Stuka" leader **Hauptmann Friedrich-Karl Freiherr von Dalwigk zu Lichtenfels**, the 33-year-old Staffelkapitän of I Gruppe, Stukageschwader 77, was shot down in his Junkers Ju.87 and killed over the sea off Portland [9 July 1940]. The kill was claimed by Pilot Officer David Moore Crook, flying a Spitfire from RAF Warmwell. Von Dalwigk, who had joined the Luftwaffe in 1933, would be posthumously awarded the Knight's Cross [21 July 1940].

V1 flying bombs — eight "Ski-site" concrete ramps, intended for the launching of flying-bombs into and over Dorset, were destroyed on the Cherbourg peninsula by bombers protected by escort fighters that took off or landed back at RAF Hurn [December 1943].

In the event no V1s would land in Dorset because their launch sites were overrun during the Battle of Normandy.

Mark VI Mosquito night-fighters from RAF Hurn, flown by Canadians of 125 (Newfoundland) Squadron and 604 (City of Edmonton) Squadron flew Anti-Diver sorties against incoming Doodlebug launch sites, [summer 1944].

V2 rockets — watched on launching from the Hook of Holland by men of the 1st Battalion of the Dorsetshire Regiment, who were holding what they called "The Island" at Bemmel, virtually surrounded by German forces [October 1944]. The terror weapon went straight up to a height of about ten kilometres before tilting into a 45 degree trajectory, towards London.

After the war scientists from Christchurch, led by Colonel Raby, would test-fire a German V2 which they reconstructed from captured parts. It was flown northwards along the North Sea coast, from Cuxhaven, near Bremerhaven, and fell into the sea off Denmark [3 October 1945]. This was a secret test, carried out by the Signals Research and Development Establishment based at Christchurch Aerodrome and Steamer Point, Highcliffe. What would be dubbed "the first firing of a captured V2", for the benefit of the world's press [4 October 1945], was in fact the second.

Colonel Raby was the director of SRDE which was developing the first British guided weapons.

V3 Hochdruckpumpe long-range gun — emplaced in massive concrete footings at Mimoyecques, near Calais. Bombed by Mosquito night-fighters of 125 Squadron and 604 Squadron, from RAF Hurn [July 1944]. The science of this vengeance weapon had not been perfected, with its shells liable to topple erratically at speeds in excess of 3,300 feet per second, and before this was corrected the site would be overrun by the Second Canadian Corps [26 September 1944].

VZ — squadron code of 412 (Royal Canadian Air Force) Squadron, flying Mark Vb Spitfires from RAF Hurn [1-6 March 1943].

W

Waite — Halifax pilot **Ronald Waite** [born 1912], of Weymouth, brought his crippled bomber home from Holland against all odds [31 July 1942]. His gunners shot down a Junkers Ju.88 and damaged a Messerschmitt Bf.110 when the already damaged bomber was intercepted over Poortugaal, near Rotterdam. The Halifax suffered complete instrument failure and one of its gunners was killed.

Despite these multiple handicaps, the bomber managed to limp home, and the story went into the newspapers, though some doubts were later expressed about the men's account. Half a century later this would be confirmed by the discovery of the wreckage of the Junkers during the building of an office block [1994].

Ronald Waite commented: "We were a bit fed up that the RAF wouldn't believe our story, especially after they had given it to the papers. It's been on my mind for the last 52 years. The fact that the wreck has now been discovered is a vindication."

Wakeling — Hurricane flyer **Sergeant Pilot Sidney Richard Ernest Wakeling** [1919-40] of 87 Squadron, from RAF Exeter, was killed when his fighter was shot down in flames over Bradford Peverell [25 August 1940]. He was aged 21 and is buried in the RAF plot at Warmwell churchyard.

Wareham crashes — a Spitfire of 152 Squadron from RAF Warmwell plunged into the ground at Bestwall, east of the town, following a Battle of Britain dog-fight [8 August 1940]. The fuselage of K9894 ended up standing vertically, its propeller embedded in a meadow, and Sergeant Pilot Robinson had a lucky escape, jumping down on the grass.

Messerschmitt Bf.109s brought down Hurricane P3421 of 56 Squadron from RAF Boscombe Down, killing Czechoslovakian Sergeant Pilot Jaroslav Hlavac, at Manor Farm, Worgret, to the west of the town [10 October 1940].

A Bf.109 also accounted for Spitfire R6597 which crashed near Wareham [28 November 1940]. Pilot Officer A.R. Watson baled out but tore his parachute and it failed to open. His death was immediately avenged by Pilot Officer Eric "Boy" Marrs who sent the culprit Messerschmitt down in flames, into Poole Bay.

Miles Magister N3980 of 302 Squadron crashed whilst low flying near Wareham [6 May 1942].

Warmwell Aerodrome — as RAF Woodsford was renamed [July 1938], lying four miles east-south-east of Dorchester (Ordnance Survey map reference SY 760 888). Airfield pundit code: "XW". Opened and operated by Flying Training Command, its three grass runways would be transferred to 10 Group Fighter Command as a frontline coastal satellite station to RAF Middle Wallop on the Hampshire Downs, when the Battle of Britain gathered pace and intensity [6 July 1940].

The neat rows of uniform headstones to the young men of the British Empire in the RAF section of Warmwell churchyard are part of a wider tragedy. Many other pilots, flying from Dorset in the Battle of Britain, came down in the front line itself — the English Channel — which became a mass grave for the flyers of both sides. Warmwell Aerodrome provided Dorset's air defence in 1940 and the Spitfires of 152 and 609 Squadrons intercepted the bombers crossing the county en route for Bristol.

Radar and decoded German radio traffic provided the scramble warnings so that the defenders' Rolls-Royce Merlin engines were only heard when there was an enemy presence approaching. There was less scope for predicting attacks on the station's other front, the Channel shipping, where the "Stukas" from the Cherbourg peninsula had pickings at will. The situation became so desperate that the Admiralty closed the Channel to Allied convoys.

Four bombs were dropped on the station by a solitary Junkers Ju88 but there were no casualties and damage was limited to holes in the grass [26 March 1941]. Much worse was the surprise attack by three Heinkel He.111s that slipped low across the Dorset coast from Lyme Bay and followed the railway east from Dorchester [1 April 1941]. Their bombs and bullets killed ten and injured twenty. Among the dead was Sergeant Pilot Fawcett of 152 Squadron.

Warmwell was soon proclaiming itself to be "the most cosmopolitan air station in the world" as the peoples of every European nation (including the odd German connection), plus both land-masses of the Americas, were augmented by representatives from all over the British Empire. They stepped from the train at Warmwell Station and were met by a coach in the car-park opposite the Frampton Arms. This would be their closest off-duty hostelry.

The names of many of the operating squadrons proclaim ethnic origins, though with wartime attrition rates they would be reinforced by very British names and faces: Punjab (130 Squadron); Hyderabad (152 Squadron); Argentine-British (164 Squadron); Mauritius (174 Squadron); Madras Presidency (234 Squadron); Northern Rhodesia (245 Squadron); Burma (257 Squadron); Rhodesia (266 Squadron); Poznanski (302 Squadron); Czech, though not named as such (312 Squadron); Royal Canadian Air Force / Ram (401 Squadron); Royal Canadian Air Force / Winnipeg Bear (402 Squadron); Royal Canadian Air Force (403 Squadron); Royal Canadian Air Force (411 Squadron); Royal Canadian Air Force (438 Squadron); Royal Canadian Air Force (439 Squadron); Royal Canadian Air Force (440 Squadron).

By 1944, from March to August it was a very different war as RAF Warmwell doubled as Station 454 of the 474 Fighter Group of the United States Army Air Force. The Lockheed Lightning P-38J fighter-bombers of 428, 429 and 430 Squadrons now flew offensive sorties against invasion objectives and targets of opportunity — the luxury of being able to turn their attention to anything that moved.

Warmwell's 48 Lightnings would suffer severe losses in the D-Day campaign. Two were shot down whilst escorting B-26 Marauders over northern France [7 May 1944] but one of the pilots, Lieutenant Thacker, was to surprise his comrades by escaping into Spain and making it back to Warmwell after D-Day. One was lost in an accident, killing Lieutenant Kimball, as it crashed near Cheselbourne [21 May 1944]. Three were lost in low-level attacks on a bridge over the River Seine [5 June 1944] from which several of the surviving aircraft brought back tree boughs wedged in their tails.

Two or three losses per offensive sweep became the regular attrition rate, including the day when the group claimed ten of a formation of 25 Focke-Wulf 190s over north-west France [18 July 1944]. By then, however, the war had moved on, and two of the three pilots were able to bale out, with some prospect of landing behind Allied lines.

Warmwell's Americans were redeployed to a forward airfield in Normandy, as the German front-lines fell back [5 August 1944].

The RAF station at Warmwell effectively disbanded with the departure of the Central Gunnery School for Sutton Bridge, Lincolnshire [June 1945]. Official closure followed [November 1945].

Warmwell's war constantly overlaps my stories of *Dorset at War* and *Battle of Britain Dorset*. The station would, however, lose the peace. Victory in Europe resulted in closure for the station and its transition to a lunar landscape of gravel pits. Some of its buildings survive west of Crossways. The lane to West Stafford crosses the former Woodsford Heath along the undug northern edge of what was a grass airfield.

A memorial stone for the base would be unveiled in Mount Skippet Way [11 June 1989].

Warmwell crashes — started when the newly opened aerodrome was known as RAF Woodsford, with the belly-landing of Bristol Blenheim K7056 from the Home Aircraft Depot of the Royal Air Force [26 November 1937].

This was followed by the loss on landing of Hawker Audax K3086 belonging to 2 Flying training School of the RAF [12 April 1938].

There would be a spate of similar mishaps as the "Phoney War" entered its final month and the Wehrmacht prepared for the invasion of the Low Countries.

Boulton Paul Defiant L6982, operated by the Central Gunnery School which was based at Warmwell, crashed on the airfield [2 April 1940].

The following day Hawker Hind K5544, with 10 Bombing and Gunnery School, crashed on landing at Warmwell [3 April 1940].

Likewise Hind K6839, also of 10 School, had its prang on landing [24 April 1940].

K5425, another Hind belonging to 10 Bombing and Gunnery School, crashed on taking off from Warmwell [27 April 1940].

Warmwell's final "Phoney War" crash, a mile from the aerodrome, was of Fairey Seal K3480, also from 10 Bombing and Gunnery School [7 May 1940]. Three days later Hitler made his big move westwards, bringing down the Chamberlain government, and beginning the process that would establish the Luftwaffe in bases on the Cherbourg peninsula, only 70 miles from the Dorset coast.

Hurricane P3598 of 87 Squadron from RAF Exeter crash-landed close to Warmwell Aerodrome after being crippled in a Battle of Britain dog-fight [11 August 1940]. Pilot Officer Andrew McLure survived, as did his fighter.

Hurricanes P3870 and P2910 of 56 Squadron from RAF Boscombe Down force-landed at Warmwell Aerodrome, though without major damage, on the day the Luftwaffe blitzed Sherborne [30 September 1940].

Hurricane V6758 of 238 Squadron from RAF Chilbolton made a forced-landing on a snow-covered Warmwell Aerodrome after icing-up at night over Portland [4 January 1941]. Pilot Officer Bob Doe survived, with eye injuries, but his fighter was ripped apart as it careered into oil-drums.

The next Hurricane in trouble, carrying the "GZ" of 32 Squadron, also attempted a forced-landing but slewed wildly out of control and crashed into the ammunition dump [11 November 1941]. The pilot and two soldiers of the Dorsetshire Regiment, on guard duty, died in the explosion.

There would be a crop of mid-air crashes on and around Warmwell Aerodrome.

Westland Whirlwind P7014 of 263 Squadron crashed while attempting to take-off [8 October 1942].

Hawker Typhoon R8823 of 266 Squadron overshot the runway on landing at Warmwell [27 October 1942].

The following year 263 Squadron experienced a chapter of crashes and other mishaps at and over RAF Warmwell, involving six of its Westland Whirlwinds.

P6991 crashed on take-off [9 February 1943].

P7057 crashed on landing [7 May 1943].

P7059 had its emergency when the engine caught fire as it was flying above the base [22 May 1943].

P7110 crashed while attempting a forced-landing near the airfield [13 July 1943].

P6981 crashed on landing at Warmwell [1 August 1943].

P7096 also crashed on landing [10 September 1943].

Tragedy marred Warmwell's welcome for the 474th Fighter Group of the United States Army Air Force, arriving with their P-38 Lightnings, when one of four RAF Typhoons of 263 Squadron spun out of a low roll and crashed half a mile west of the airfield. Pilot Officer Graham Smith was killed as HHS MN129 exploded [15.00 hours, 12 March 1944].

Watercombe crash — of Spitfire N3238 belonging to 609 Squadron from RAF Warmwell, at Watercombe Farm, between Warmwell and Owermoigne, which had been crippled by Messerschmitt Bf.109s over Weymouth [7 October 1940]. Pilot Officer Alan Norman Feary baled out, but at a height that was too low for his parachute to open.

Watson — Spitfire flyer **Pilot Officer Arthur Roy Watson** [1921-40] of 152 Squadron from RAF Warmwell claimed a Heinkel He.111 bomber when the Dorset fighters were drafted eastwards for the air defence of London [15 September 1940]. He fell to his death near Wareham after engagements with Messerschmitt Bf.109s over Poole Bay [28 November 1940]. He was seen to have "bungled his baling out and tore his parachute" which "streamed out behind him but owing to the tears did not open". Pilot Officer Eric "Boy" Marrs then crept up on the culprit Bf.109, in his blind spot, and avenged Watson's death with "the easiest victory I've had". Watson's body was not recovered.

Welham — RAF **Aircraftman L.W. Welham** [died 15 August 1941], is buried at Langton Herring, in the churchyard extension above Lantern Cottage. He was aged 21.

West Knighton crashes — at Little Mayne Farm, of Flight Lieutenant J.C. Kennedy's Hurricane of 238 Squadron from Middle Wallop, Hampshire, killing the pilot after a Battle of Britain dog-fight [13 July 1940].

Typhoon HHS MN129 of 263 Squadron crashed in fields north of the village, half a mile west of Warmwell Aerodrome when it spun out of a low roll that had been staged as part of the RAF's welcome for the 474th Fighter Group of the United States Army Air Force [12 March 1944]. Pilot Officer Graham Smith was killed.

Weston — Spitfire flyer **Pilot Officer Weston** from RAF Warmwell claimed a third share of 152 Squadron's kill of a Heinkel He.111 off Portland [15 September 1940]. He delivered the coup de grâce which sent it blazing into the sea. The bomber probably belonged to Kampfgruppe 55 from Chartres.

Weymouth crashes — into the countryside, of a Dornier Do.17 shot down by Spitfires of 152 Squadron from RAF Warmwell [25 July 1940].

The first RAF fighter to be lost offshore was Spitfire N3023 of 609 Squadron from RAF Warmwell [27 July 1940].

Hurricane P3222 of 238 Squadron from RAF Middle Wallop was shot down off Weymouth by a Messerschmitt Bf.109, killing Pilot Officer Frederick Norman Cawse [11 August 1940]. He was aged 22.

A Messerschmitt Bf.109 escort fighter was put into the sea during the Luftwaffe's Adlertag (Eagle Day) attack [13 August 1940]. The kill was claimed by Pilot Officer Tadeusz Nowierski in a Spitfire of 609 Squadron. The German pilot, Leutnant Heinz Pfannschmidt, was rescued and taken prisoner.

The next Weymouth crash was British, when a crippled Hurricane crash-landed at Field Barn Farm, beside Radipole Lake [15 August 1940]. It belonged to 87 Squadron from RAF Exeter.

Spitfire N3061 of 234 Squadron fell into Weymouth Bay [6 September 1940], followed by Hurricane P3414 of 504 Squadron [30 September 1940]. Both were shot down in Battle of Britain dog-fights.

Hawker Hurricane Z4993, an adapted airframe being tested by the Aeroplane and Armament Experimental Establishment, flew into the side of Ridgeway Hill, above Upwey, when it was shrouded in hill-fog [25 October 1941].

Whitcombe crash — near Whitcombe Barn, of Hurricane P2987 belonging to 504 Squadron from RAF Filton [17.00 hours, 30 September 1940]. Damaged in the dog-fights following the Luftwaffe's blitz of Sherborne, Pilot Officer Edward Murray Frisby also found himself running out of fuel, only four miles from Warmwell Aerodrome. He was able to make a successful forced-landing on rolling chalk downland.

Wick — Luftwaffe ace **Hauptmann Helmut Wick** [1918-40], holder of the Iron Cross First Class, who had 57 white kill-bars painted on the rudder of his Messerschmitt Bf.109E, was shot down over the sea by Flight-Lieutenant John Dundas of 609 Squadron from RAF Warmwell [28 November 1940]. "I've finished an Me.109 — whoopee," were the last words heard from Dundas as he then disappeared into radio silence, off the Isle of Wight. Neither body was recovered.

Wildblood — Spitfire flyer **Pilot Officer Timothy Seddon Wildblood** [1920 - 40] claimed a Messerschmitt Bf.109 [11 August 1940], followed by a Bf.110 [12 August 1940], then a Junkers Ju.87 and a half share in another Ju.87 the same day [18 August 1940].

He was reported "Missing in Action" after being lost over the sea in R6994 during a day of fierce Battle of Britain dog-fights [25 August 1940]. His body was not recovered.

Williams — Spitfire flyer **Pilot Officer William Dudley Williams** [1915-76] served with 152 Squadron at RAF Warmwell and claimed a total of five enemy aircraft during the Battle of Britain. He was awarded the Distiguished Flying Cross [7 January 1941].

He would become an instructor and then returned to combat in the Far East, commanding 615 Squadron from Feni, India [1943]. Though he died in Sussex he had maintained his love of Dorset and is buried at West Knighton, only a mile from the former Warmwell Aerodrome.

"ONE OF THE FEW", his gravestone reads.

Wills — glider pilot **Philip Wills** was towed by an ancient Avro 504 biplane into the middle of the English Channel, and released in a German Minimos glider to drift back to the Purbeck cliffs at St Alban's Head,

Worth Matravers [23 June 1940]. The object of the exercise, which was successfully accomplished on behalf of the Telecommunications Research Establishment, was to ensure that current radar technology would pick up signals from the wooden gliders of any German invasion force.

Window — codename for radar-reflective foil, deployed from the air in the form of millions of strips of aluminium foil, developed by the Telecommunications Research Establishment at Worth Matravers. Perfected in Dorset by radar pioneer Robert Watson-Watt [winter 1941-42] it was devised to create a smoke-screen effect upon enemy radar sets at the onset of mass bombing raids. Fighter Command blocked its operational use, however, fearing that it might give the Germans the idea at a time when they were still able to carry out major air attacks against Britain.

"Let us open the window," Prime Minister Winston Churchill eventually decided, and it was first used in an air raid on Hamburg [24 - 25 July 1943] by 791 British bombers. Forty tons were dropped — a total of 92 million strips — and all but twelve of the aircraft returned. Normally the losses from such a raid would have been about 48, so the use of Window had saved 36 aeroplanes and their crews.

Winfrith Heath Decoy Aerodrome — rigged with flares and moving lights to draw air attack from RAF Warmwell, being three miles south-east from the actual airfield. It added a Junkers Ju.88, apparently brought down by anti-aircraft fire, to its collection of bomb craters [4 May 1941]. The crew were able to bale out safely.

Winfrith Newburgh crashes — having clashed with Messerschmitt Bf.109 and Bf.110 fighters over Bournemouth, Pilot Officer Kenneth Marston of 56 Squadron from RAF Boscombe Down managed to bring damaged Hurricane P2866 down at Longcutts East, East Knighton, in a crash-landing [11.30 hours, 30 September 1940]. It was the day that the Luftwaffe blitzed Sherborne. Marston survived, with shrapnel wounds and minor cuts, but would lose his life at the end of the year when a fighter overshot the runway at RAF Middle Wallop and sliced through his tail [12 December 1940].

A Junkers Ju.88, apparently hit by anti-aircraft fire, crashed on the decoy-airfield that had been established on Winfrith Heath to draw the Luftwaffe from RAF Warmwell [4 May 1941]. The crew were able to bale out safely.

Spitfire P8656 of 234 Squadron crashed at West Knighton [14 July 1941].

Wings over Dorset — book title of the county's first gloriously illustrated flying history, compiled by Poole glider pilot Leslie Dawson [1983]. It is subtitled *"Aviation's story in the South"* and the present author contributed several sections and the captions. I also produced the book for him, through Dorset Publishing Company.

The revised edition would have even more pictures [1989].

Winkton Advanced Landing Ground — in the Avon valley, extending from Winkton in the parish of Burton and north to Ripley, near Christchurch (Ordnance Survey map reference SZ 169 971). Elevation 40 feet above sea level. Hedges were grubbed out and two runways were laid as sheets of steel mesh directly on to the grass [July 1943].

Four blister hangars were erected. Officially opened in March 1944 and handed over to the United States Army Air Force, though nominally under 11 Group RAF Fighter Command. One runway ran north-south from east of Parsonage Farm to west of Clockhouse Farm, and the other east-west from the Ripley road to within a third of a mile of cottages at Bransgore.

Used as a satellite airfield to Christchurch, principally for cross-Channel ground-attack missions. Closed when the war began to move into Germany [January 1945]. Pundit code "XT".

Winterborne Houghton crash — on Great Hill, the downland above Meriden Wood, of Hurricane V6777 belonging to 238 Squadron from RAF Chilbolton [16.00 hours, 7 October 1940]. It was gunned down by Messerschmitt Bf.109s which had been escorting bombers attacking the Westland Aircraft Company at Yeovil.

Pilot Officer Aubrey Richard Covington baled out over Dorset for the second time in a week — apparently the first occasion was near Sherborne after accounting for two Messerschmitt Bf.110s [1 October 1940].

The second time he was not quite unscathed, being taken to Blandford Cottage Hospital for treatment of minor injuries.

Wolton — Spitfire flyer **Pilot Officer Ralph "Bob" Wolton** [born 1914] claimed the first two kills for 152 Squadron from RAF Warmwell [25 July 1940]. One was a Dornier and the other a Junkers Ju.87 "Stuka". The gunner of another "Stuka" would shoot down Wolton's Spitfire, into Lyme Bay, three weeks later [15 August 1940]. He managed to swim to one of the offshore marked buoys of the Chesil Beach Bombing Range, from which he was rescued by an RAF launch from Lyme Regis.

Nearly plunged to his death after losing control in a dive [7 September 1940]. Though he baled out of the Spitfire at 13,000 feet above Dorchester, he did not manage to sort out the cords and activate the chute until only a thousand feet from the ground.

Picked off one of the Junkers Ju.88s that wrecked the Vickers Supermarine Works at Woolston, Southampton — the main centre for Spitfire production — with 70 tons of bombs [26 September 1940]. The kill fell into the sea off the Isle of Wight.

Posted to the Central Flying School, Upavon, to become an instructor. Then taught Polish pilots, at Newton, and was later attached to 417 Squadron of the United States Army Air Force, training them to fly British Beaufighter night-fighters.

Survived the war and retired from the RAF as Flight Lieutenant [1948].

Woodsford Aerodrome — RAF Woodsford, a grass airfield of three runways at 207-feet above sea level on a gravel plain four miles east-south-east of Dorchester (Ordnance Survey map reference SY 760 885) was established by Flying Training Command for its School of Air Firing [May 1937]. Renamed RAF Warmwell, in which parish it also lies, because unlike Woodsford that has an identifiable and findable village [July 1938].

Wool crash — Brigadier D.V.L. Allott, the Commandant of the Royal Armoured Corps Centre, was killed in a helicopter crash at Bovington Camp [14 May 1969].

Wootton Fitzpaine crash — north of the road to Mónkton Wyld, of Hurricane N2434 of 56 Squadron from RAF Boscombe Down, during dog-fights following the Luftwaffe attack on Sherborne [16.30 hours, 30 September 1940]. Though wounded in his right knee, Sergeant Pilot Peter Hutton Fox was able to bale out successfully.

Worth Aerodrome — known as Swanage Aerodrome, opened with a flying display [16 August 1928] and was located on The Plain between Worth Matravers village and St Alban's Head. Inspired and maintained by veteran flyer Lieutenant-Colonel Louis Strange who lived at Worth.

Worth Matravers — RAF Worth Matravers [1942-70] came into being in buildings vacated by the Telecommunications Research Establishment, as a link in the Gee Chain navigation system. Its ten national transmitting stations, operating in pairs, provided accurately timed radio pulses. Differences in arrival time between the signals enabled the aircraft's position to be determined by intersecting hyperbolic lines on a pre-printed Gee lattice chart.

The system "revolutionised the effectiveness of RAF bombing raids" with "targets being found and bombed as never before". By the late 1960s, however, the Ministry of Defence announced that other ground-based navigation aids and airborne systems had effectively replaced Gee, leading to the standing down of the system and demolition of its tall aerials.

No.407 Signals Unit operated from the Purbeck station.

Worth Matravers crashes — Miles Magister P6362 of 32 Maintenance Unit of the Royal Air Force dived into the top of the Purbeck cliffs half a mile south-west of the Telecommunications Research Establishment, in a field on the north side of Emmetts Hill [14 September 1940].

Messerschmitt Bf.109 belonging to Lehrgeschwader 2, a unit testing improved aircraft under operational conditions, came down following engine failure whilst on a weather reconnaissance flight [30 November 1940]. Unteroffizier Paul Wacker belly-landed at Woodyhyde Farm. The tail section of his machine survives, having been used to repair the captured test-flown Bf.109 that is now in the Royal Air Force Museum, at Hendon.

Wellington X9677 of 218 Squadron from RAF Marham, Norfolk, crashed into the sea off St Alban's Head whilst on a bombing mission to Bordeaux [10-11 October 1941]. Three members of the crew were picked up by lifeboat but the other three drowned.

Hit by anti-aircraft fire from an escort vessel, Luftwaffe ace Oberleutnant Werner Machold, Staffelkapitän of the 7th Gruppe of Jagdeschwader 2 Richthofen, turned his Messerschmitt Bf.109E landwards and successfully crash-landed among the stone workings at Worth Matravers [6 June 1941]. He was taken into captivity and ditto his fighter, for inspection by the Royal Aircraft Establishment, Farnborough, on account of its improved Zusatz-gear mechanism which fed nitrous oxide to boost the engine power.

WX — squadron code of 302 (Poznanski) Squadron, flying Mark IIb Hurricanes [5 September - 11 October 1941] and then Mark Vb Spitfires [27 April - 1 May 1942], from RAF Warmwell.

Wynford Eagle crash — at Shatcombe Farm, of Spitfire N3039 from RAF Warmwell, which had been crippled by enemy fighters following the Luftwaffe attack on the Westland Aircraft Factory at Yeovil [16.30 hours, 7 October 1940]. It burst into flames on impact and though he was pulled from the wreckage Pilot Officer Harold John Akroyd of 152 Squadron, based at RAF Warmwell, died the following day from burns.

Mosquito: some were produced at Christchurch,
with Dorset's operational version being the
night-fighters based at RAF Hurn in 1944

X

XC — pundit code for RAF Christchurch, on ten feet high white letters at the airfield and flashed at night in red light Morse code, from a Pundit mobile beacon some miles from the station.

X-Gerät — known also as Wotan I, being the German radio direction beam used by pathfinders of Kampfgruppe 100 [1940-41], against which countermeasures were successfully developed by the Telecommunications Research Establishment, Worth Matravers, in time to foil a raid that would have devastated the crucial Rolls-Royce aero engine works at Derby [8 May 1942].

XM — squadron code of 182 Squadron, flying rocket-firing Typhoons on cross-Channel missions from RAF Hurn [1 April - 20 June 1944].

XP — squadron code of 174 (Mauritius) Squadron, flying Mark IIb Hurricane "Hurri-bombers" from RAF Warmwell [1-21 September 1942].

XT — pundit code, in letters on the ground and in Morse code lights at night, of RAF/USAAF Advance Landing Ground Winkton, near Christchurch.

XW — pundit code for RAF Warmwell, on ten feet high white letters at the airfield and flashed at night in red light Morse code, from a Pundit mobile beacon some miles from the station.

**Oxford: twin-engined trainer, built for
the RAF by Airspeed at Christchurch**

Y

Y-Gerät — also known as Wotan II, being the German radio direction target finding system deployed across Dorset by the pathfinding 3rd Gruppe of Kampfgeschwader 26, whose aircraft carried the cross on the rear fuselage [1940-42]. It transmitted from the Hague peninsula, north-west of Cherbourg, on 42.4 megacycles.

YO — squadron code of 401 (RCAF Ram) Squadron, briefly flying Mark IXb Spitfires from RAF Warmwell [24 October - 4 November 1944].

Thunderbolt: P-47 fighters of the United States Army Air Force took over the grass runways of RAF Christchurch to support the Normandy landings, with cross-Channel sorties in 1944

Z

Zeals Aerodrome — just over the Wiltshire border, a mile north-east of Bourton which is Dorset's most northerly parish (Ordnance Survey map reference ST 780 330). Provided by the Air Ministry for 10 Group Fighter Command [May 1942] and then handed over to the United States Army Air Force [August 1943].

British night-fighters continued to operate from it and were active above Dorset, with coverage being provided by the Mark XIII Mosquitoes of 488 (New Zealand) Squadron [12 May - 29 July 1944], 410 Squadron [18 June - 28 July 1944] and 604 Squadron [25-28 July 1944].

Then, with the local war moving eastwards, and the new priority being the training of aircraft-carrier flight crews for the Japanese conflict, the base was passed to the Fleet Air Arm and was named HMS *Humming Bird* [April 1945]. It closed as soon as the last ships returned from the Pacific [January 1946]. Pundit code "ZL".

Zero — type of Admiralty airship, based in Dorset during the latter part of the Great War, [1917-18], with mooring stations at Upton, in the parish of Lytchett Minster, and on the hills above Powerstock.

ZH — squadron code of 266 (Rhodesia) Squadron, flying rocket-firing Typhoons on cross-Channel missions from RAF Hurn [13-20 July 1944].

Zurakowski — Spitfire pilot **Pilot Officer Janusz Zurakowski** [born 1914] transferred from 234 Squadron to 609 Squadron at RAF Middle Wallop [4 October 1940] and was then stationed at RAF Warmwell. Survived the war, leaving the service as Squadron Leader, and became a test pilot for Gloster Aircraft [1950] and then chief test pilot for Avro's Canadian division [1952] where he settled.

ZY — squadron code of 247 (China-British) Squadron, flying rocket-firing Typhoons on cross-Channel missions from RAF Hurn [24 April - 20 June 1944].

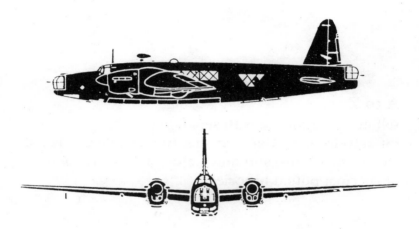

Wellington: flights over The Fleet, behind Chesil Beach, tested the prototype bouncing bomb that would breach the Ruhr dams in 1943

A to Z
self-indexing format with separate entries
for aerodromes, codes, crashes (under relevant parish),
flyers, squadrons, and much else – in a succession
of succinct potted histories